Online Business Resouces

Paul Galloway

MADE E-Z PRODUCTS™ Inc.
Deerfield Beach, Florida / www.MadeE-Z.com

Online Business Resources Made E-Z™
© Copyright 2001-2002 Made E-Z Products, Inc.
Printed in the United States of America

 384 South Military Trail
Deerfield Beach, FL 33442

http://www.MadeE-Z.com
All rights reserved.

2 3 4 5 6 7 8 9 10

This publication is designed to provide accurate and authoritative information in regard to subject matter covered. It is sold with the understanding that neither the publisher nor author is engaged in rendering legal, accounting, or other professional services. If legal advice or other expert assistance is required, the services of a competent professional should be sought. From: *A Declaration of Principles jointly adopted by a Committee of the American Bar Association and a Committee of Publishers.*

Online Business Resources Made E-Z™

Paul Galloway

Limited warranty and disclaimer

This self-help product is intended to be used by the consumer for his/her own benefit. It may not be reproduced in whole or in part, resold, or used for commercial purposes without written permission from the publisher.

This product is designed to provide authoritative and accurate information in regard to the subject matter covered. However, the accuracy of the information is not guaranteed, as laws and regulations may change or be subject to differing interpretations. Consequently, you may be responsible for following alternative procedures, or using material different from those supplied with this product.

Neither the author, publisher, distributor nor retailer are engaged in rendering legal, accounting or other professional services. Accordingly, the publisher, author, distributor and retailer shall have neither liability nor responsibility to any party for any loss or damage caused or alleged to be caused by the use of this product.

Copyright notice

The purchaser of this book is hereby authorized to reproduce in any form or by any means electronic or mechanical, including photocopying, all forms and documents contained in this book, provided it is for non-profit, educational or private use. Such reproduction requires no further permission from the publisher and/or payment of any permission fee.

The reproduction of any form or document in any other publication intended for sale is prohibited without the written permission of the publisher. Publication for non-profit use should provide proper attribution to Made E-Z Products, Inc.™

ABOUT THE AUTHOR

Paul Galloway graduated from Brigham Young University with a Bachelor's degree in Electronics Engineering Technology. After college, he worked for Motorola as an electrical engineer.

While employed at Motorola, he developed his own web site to provide small/home business products. This profitable web site still operates and can be found at http://www.palis.com. While maintaining his web site, he taught himself Internet programming and soon expanded his business to include creating software for other Internet marketers.

In 1998, he created one of the first "affiliate program" software packages for small business owners called *Your Own Affiliate Program* which is available on his web site. While his online business grew, he wrote his first book, *Marketing Alchemy*. Pressured by popular demand from satisfied customers, he developed a more sophisticated application—*Synergyx*—which was the first Internet application to include an affiliate program, shopping cart, and digital product delivery system in an integrated package.

Presently, Mr. Galloway serves as the chief technical officer for ADNet International, an Internet marketing and promotion firm. Although based in Chico, California, Paul Galloway works as a "telecommuter" from his home in Ocala, Florida. He is married and has one son.

Table of Contents

Introduction 7
1   Business philosophy 11
2   Advertising and promotion 19
3   Affiliate programs 67
4   Communications 79
5   Data and equipment protection 93
6   Discussion groups and diversions 105
7   Ebook software 111
8   Efficiency/productivity boosters 117
9   Email related tools and resources 125
10   Ezines (electronic magazines) 133
11   Fulfillment, help sites, & Internet marketing 143
12   Joint ventures 151
13   Legal resources 169
14   Miscellaneous 187
15   Online payment methods 201
16   Promotional items, premiums, and incentives 215
17   Research and strategic intelligence 221
18   Search engine positioning 253
19   Web site design/hosting resources 265
20   Web site promotion 301
21   Web site software resources 321
      Index 327

Introduction to Online Business Resources Made E-Z™

Two years ago I wrote a book about using the newest technology tools to improve every aspect of your business. The book was well received, and the great majority of my customers singled out the "resource section" as their favorite part. Indeed, I believe I could have sold the contents of that section alone for the price of the entire book.

Since then, I have observed the creation of many more tools which, when used properly, give you a tremendous advantage in the marketplace. I knew eventually I'd need to do a completely new book.

With that end in mind, I have "bookmarked" over 2100 web sites, kept hundreds of "resource-rich" emails, torn out and filed advertisements from numerous magazines, and littered my workplace with a multitude of "post-it" notes. This guide is the culmination of those 2 years of "keeping my eyes peeled" for business tools. I will show you what they are, how to use them, and where to get them. You'll be surprised how powerful and inexpensive some of these tools are.

There are two ways to use this guide. I believe anyone can/will discover a number of useful (and previously unknown) resources just by browsing the table of contents and turning to the pages of interest—or by scanning the guide from cover to cover.

One of the sections I'd recommend *everyone* read carefully is the one about data protection. I have found most people are woefully uninformed about this topic until after they've lost days, weeks, or months of their critical business data and creative work. Yes, it *can* happen to you.

Rather than organizing this guide as a typical book with "chapters," I have elected to list the various resources (and relevant commentary) alphabetically—I believe this is a more intuitive and usable approach.

Though these tools are powerful, they are not to be used by themselves. They are extensions or enhancements of long-practiced and proven direct marketing methods. Given the importance of direct marketing fundamentals to the successful use of these tools, I have included an overview of "direct marketing fundamentals" as an appendix.

This guide is not an internet promotion or about web site design. Neither is it a "how to make money on the internet" or a "doing business on the internet" book.

While I include *many* links/resources relevant to these topics, this *is* a resource guide—containing listings and commentary about tools and resources which will aid business owners in every aspect of their business (online and offline).

- These links are not listed in any particular order within a category. A resource listed first in a category is not necessarily any better than the resource listed last in that same category.
- These links are not all-inclusive. First, even though I spend 10-16 hours a day online, I doubt I have seen all the links/resources for any particular topic. Second, I have purposely omitted some of the high priced services (if there were viable alternatives at lower cost), or services/products which do not divulge their prices right up front.
- I have sifted through thousands of links/resources before settling on the ones here. I have tried my best to include only resources from reputable companies offering good value for the money. I have often relied on the recommendations of other online business owners whom I know.

Introduction

However, since I haven't personally used *all* of these services, their inclusion here does not constitute a personal endorsement or guarantee on my part. It is still your responsibility to check out each service for yourself and make sure it fits well with your needs.

- The internet is a very dynamic place. Links change frequently. In many cases I have linked directly to a specific product/service of a company, rather than their "home page." It's quite likely that a number of these pages, over time, will be moved to other places on the company site. If you try a link and get a "file not found" message, try "backing up." To illustrate, suppose you tried this link:

    http://www.companyname.com/products/thisproduct

If the link yielded a "file not found" error, the next thing you should try is this:

http://www.companyname.com/products

There would very likely be a listing of the various products sold by "companyname.com" on this page. If *that* doesn't work, then your final option is to try the company's "home" page:

http://www.companyname.com

Unless the company has folded completely, this page should include links to their "products," "services," "solutions," etc.

Note: A few of these links are to products and services for which I am enrolled in an "affiliate program." This means if you end up purchasing one of these products after "clicking through" the link I provide, I will get a referral fee. There has been some discussion online of late as to whether or not authors should do this. No consensus has been reached on the issue, but I feel as long as I inform you up front, it's okay.

Business philosophy

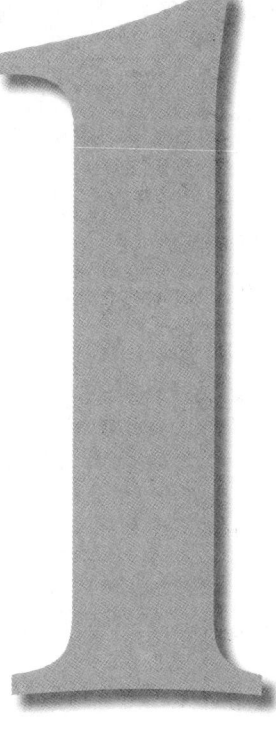

Business philosophy

Okay, I admit this first section is not about resources, it's about my own personal philosophies related to business. I've wanted to say something along these lines for some time now, and this is my chance—be warned, it borders on "religious" in nature. I hope you won't begrudge me this personal indulgence.

The Golden Rule

I was raised in a Christian home, and one of the first "religious" things I remember learning was the "Golden Rule." Interestingly enough, I didn't learn it first at church—I learned it on an episode of the television show "Daniel Boone." In this particular episode, Boone was teaching his son about the "Golden Rule" and how it should be applied to the Indian tribes in the area.

As I learned it, the Golden Rule was taken from the New Testament:

"...whatsoever ye would that men should do to you, do ye even so to them."
(Matthew 7:12)

Christianity certainly has no monopoly on this principle—there are similar admonitions in the religions of Buddhism, Hinduism, Confucianism, Islam, Judaism, Sikhism, Taoism, Jainism, Zoroastrianism—and probably others as well.

I believe "you reap what you sow" is another closely related principle. It has also been described as "what goes around comes around" and "the cosmic law of cause and effect." Basically this principle says any action you take will have consequences. If the action is "good" or "positive," the consequences of that action (which are reflected back to you) will likewise be "good" or "positive." If the action is "bad" or "negative," that's what you'll get back.

Taken together, these two principles basically say "Treat others as you would like to be treated, and others will treat you as you'd like." That's not to say everyone will treat you positively. Everyone has the agency to act as they please. However, if you're dishing out positive experiences, that's generally what you'll get back.

> **note** Treat your customers with respect, courtesy, and genuine consideration—they'll respond with loyalty, referrals, and long-lasting relationships.

It's my belief these two guiding principles can and should be applied to your business, and the rest of your life as well.

No substitute for integrity

We're living in an age where it's not "popular" to be a "goodie-goodie" (someone who is concerned with and strives to do "the right thing"). Ethical considerations have given way to legal rationalizations. The predominant thinking seems to be "if it's legal, it's okay to do it—whether it really helps the customer or not is of no concern."

However, when we want/need help, we all look for someone we can trust, a "straight shooter." We go to someone we know will help us without gouging us, someone who will tell us if they can't provide what we really need, rather than taking our money and selling us something that doesn't really do what we require.

Chapter 1

Be that kind of person, and people *will* come to you. I've had a number of experiences where I have suggested to a potential client their needs might be better met by a competitor's product, but they ordered my product instead *because* I was honest enough to tell them about my competitor's product, even at the risk of losing the sale.

> **note** Be warned: anything you do that is the least bit deceptive will reduce your credibility.

Some sales letters tiptoe around the truth to increase the bottom-line—they don't actually *state* an untruth, but they use clever wording to cause the reader to believe. Here's an example:

In order to get customers to "act now," some sales letters I've seen on the web recently have used a "hard" deadline set for the current date: "this offer *absolutely ends* (today's date)." When the next day rolls around, the date of the deadline changes! It's a moving deadline because there's no real deadline, the marketer just wants to give the appearance of scarcity because people will be more likely to buy now if they believe the product has limited availability.

Well, that's the definition of "deception," "to cause one to believe an untruth." Some people will be fooled by this and will buy. Other people, however, will see right through this scheme and, because the marketer shows a willingness to deceive people in order to line his pockets with their money, will not buy the product in question.

Here are some other examples of credibility-reducing behavior:

- **Making exaggerated claims.** I recently read a sales letter for a software product similar to the one I sell. In it, the marketer gushed "…nobody has even half of the benefits of (product name)." I don't think this was an act of purposeful deception—I think the marketer just got caught up in his own hype. However, the claim was absolutely without merit, and as such, severely undermined this marketer's credibility.

- **Disguising the truth.** I remember a well-known internet marketer explaining how to use his newest software tool. As part of this explanation, he talked about how "as far as he knew," his software was the only one with a particular feature.

  But I knew there were several software packages with that same feature. He was lying, purposely avoided looking at any of the competing products, or he just hadn't taken time to see what was available. In any case, "Bye-bye credibility, it was nice to know you."

- **Pretending to be someone you're not.** It's sad, but I've seen a number of posts at online discussion groups where someone is asking how to do marketing on the internet. I follow their link to their home page, and guess what they're selling? Their own information product or consultation about the very subject they were asking for help with! Can you say "the blind leading the blind"?

Relationships are what matter

Generally, making a bunch of "one time" sales is *not* the way to build your business. To be successful you need to cultivate your relationship with your customers.

Send them emails, postcards, and special offers. Call them on the phone once in a while and find out how they're doing. If you are sincerely interested in *their* well being and success, and you show this with your actions, your customers will always come to you first when they have need of something. Not only this, but some of them may very well become your personal friends.

Your sincerity is important. To begin with, you may be just "going through the motions" of keeping in contact with your customers—because it's a good business practice. But if you talk to your customers regularly, you really will develop an interest in their well being—and they'll know it.

Chapter 1

A big part of cultivating your customer relationships is your availability. Don't hide behind a P.O. box and voice-mail number. Make yourself available (schedule customer service time for yourself if necessary) to answer their questions.

Well, that's it. I truly believe if you will implement the above ideas in your business, you'll have a much better chance of being successful. Certainly a better chance than if you don't!

Advertising and promotion

Advertising and promotion

Just to be sure there's no misunderstanding, the resources in this section are related to online advertising and promotion. The only exception are the "Press Release" resources, which could be used for online or offline advertising.

I'm fortunate to be working with two of the top minds in the internet advertising industry, Patrick Anderson and Michael Henderson of ADNet International. They have been kind enough to let me include one of their excellent articles on the subject of "Internet Advertising."

Advertise...LIKE YOU MEAN IT!

How 2 guys sold over $620,000.00 in 7 short weeks

By Patrick Anderson & Michael Henderson

We recorded a three-hour training session with our staff that outlined the step-by-step advertising method Michael and I use for ourselves and our prominent "dot com" clients. No useless theory. This is a set of guerrilla advertising techniques learned from four years of being in the trenches, while being pressured by clients to *perform!*

In the past, these "killer" advertising strategies have only been shared with people who have signed non-compete non-disclosure agreements with us. When I showed my business manager the draft of this update to our book he stopped and stared at me. "Do you *really* want to give all of this away?" he frowned. "I mean, anyone could just use this for themselves. You've told them *everything.*"

That's right. I've held nothing back.

What you are about to read are transcripts from a three-hour intensive training session that I gave to my staff the second week in December. I was launching a new promotion and I wanted their brains engaged.

My good friend, Stephen Mahaney, called me that night and I shared what I was doing with him. We worked on the project together for about four hours and launched our programs the next morning.

The results were instantaneous!

We had done our homework and followed the formula that I explain in the first chapter of our book. We determined what people wanted to buy and looked at how others were selling it. Then we got our website and added an opt-in list. We bought from ourselves to make sure the sales process worked. Then we wrote advertisements and placed our ads everywhere.

That's it—50 days later we had sold $620,562.50 completely online! That's over $12,000 per day. Neither one of us had to worry about order fulfillment or inventory. All we did was advertise effectively.

Stephen had the benefit of having already created a large, responsive opt-in list. This gave him a huge boost over us. Our existing list is small compared to his, so we made 5 times *less* than he did originally. So we had to rely on joint ventures and advertising to extend our reach and deliver our message to a larger group of people.

Chapter 2

Here's the moral of the story. After 7 weeks we had outsold Stephen—even though he had a huge jump start with his own list. Our out-of-pocket costs were only $4,320.47, and our sales were over 82 times that amount!

Here's the part that is going to blow you away. I hired a 28 year old "kid" who was working at Blockbuster and taught him how to do this for us. I was busy with other stuff, so I did *none* of the advertising myself. I simply showed Robert my strategies. He applied the knowledge I am about to share with you. No disrespect to Robert—he is very bright and there is nothing wrong with working at Blockbuster. My point is that he had *no* previous Internet marketing experience. Think about it.

Here's what Stephen Mahaney wrote in his newsletter:

"Patrick and Michael really know how to make money on the Internet, *and* they know how to teach others how to make money on the Internet! A rare combination. In fact, they are so good at teaching that my last brainstorming session with Patrick produced over $100,000 profit for yours truly in 6 weeks. If I didn't know them I'd be skeptical. Trouble is, I do know them. It is possible. After all, I have an extra $100,000+ in my pocket because of these guys.

Now, before you start looking for that new Ferrari, it's only fair to remind you that your mileage may vary. After all, I don't know what your abilities are, nor can I predict your dedication and willingness to work. Realize also that I didn't start from scratch on my way to that 100 grand. I had a head start. After all, I've been on the Internet for over four years now. My company is already profitable, and I also have a clue about how the net works. Regardless, the fact remains that Patrick and Michael's information is 100% responsible for my quick $100,000+ profit."

That's quite an endorsement! But I'm sure you are going to thank us in the same way when you start to apply these ideas and make money for yourself.

OK, without further ado, let's start rolling that in-house training tape and you can listen in as I hammer the principles of online advertising into the heads of my staff. If it sounds like I'm being very insistent with them, it is because I really wanted them to *get it!* Remember—at the time I gave this training session I *really* cared about the promotion I was about to kick off. You should care about your business with the same amount of passion.

What you absolutely MUST know about Internet advertising!

This information is based on actual results and is an outgrowth of four years of successfully launching start-up Internet businesses.

I'm about to show you what it takes to advertise on the web and get enough response to actually make money with your ad dollars.

First, a little terminology. "Buying media" is the process of paying a website owner to put up a banner or sending a check to an ezine editor to run your classified ad. Websites and ezines are the "media" and you are the advertiser.

I joke about "professional" media buyers who cannot advertise well. In fact, I despise them! Many agencies and media buying companies spend ad money while convincing their clients that they are "branding." I think "branding" is a lame coverup word to use when you've run a direct response campaign that doesn't work.

Now you know where I'm coming from. All advertising should net you a return on your investment. It should be a fixed cost of doing business that is spent in order to increase sales. You are spending money to *make* money.

Chapter 2

MOST Internet marketing "experts" DO NOT know how to advertise!

All the Internet marketing experts whom I know are not advertisers. They aren't placing media for their clients everyday. They aren't doing major national campaigns. They aren't spending hundreds of thousands of dollars over the course of a year for a client, while actually being concerned with the return of the response.

note — You can't sell product the same way that you sell information and marketing books. They are two different things.

Most Internet marketers write books and make tapes. They have learned how to sell information products on the web. It's great to take their advice if that's what you're doing.

Internet marketers are involved in selling personality, and they are like a star shop. Their name and their particular style of writing is what they sell. People get introduced to them, know them, like them, and trust them. But that's different from the way that you approach selling products. With products, there's no personality. There's brand perhaps (that's why starting with brand name products helps your sales), but to introduce personality on top of product is tough.

There is another big difference. Internet marketers typically are selling their information products at 10 times what it costs them to produce it. They have huge margins so they don't need huge sales. Products typically have lower margins. You have people involved in the distribution chain who need to make money, so your percentage of money to be made will be smaller. Therefore, it matters to you a lot more how you advertise. You've got to work off of volume and the advertising has got to create enough volume so you can create a return on your investment.

All of the prominent "dot com" companies are spending ridiculous amounts on advertising that doesn't work. Value America reported $57.6

25

million in revenue and $31.6 million in losses (quarter ended 9/30/99). For the same quarter, PlanetRx.com reported $3.1 million in revenue and $26.7 million in losses.

There is *no* entrepreneur who can be in business very long making $3,000 a month while it costs them $27,000 to get there. It won't happen for more than a month. What you've got to understand is how to push and tweak the Internet, how to squeeze every nickel out of your ad dollars, and that's what this strategy session is going to be about.

The point of buying media is to get additional reach and exposure for your message—and to generate traffic. Not just traffic to your site, but traffic to a sales process. You want to find a targeted consumer with an interest in purchasing something, then deliver the rest of the offer (the incentive and premiums to make them buy today) and move them to the order form. You don't care about anything else except getting their email address and name.

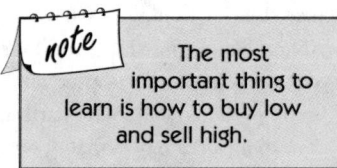
The most important thing to learn is how to buy low and sell high.

A key thing to understand is that many people don't know what they're doing on the Internet. Then there are the "ad salesmen" who are hustlers and sharks. Those are the first two groups of people you are going to run into when you're attempting to buy media.

To recap, the goal of all your advertising promotion is:

- To pay as little as possible.

- To get sales.

- To get names for your opt-in list.

Chapter 2

When you're setting out to do this you have to look at where you want your customer base to come from. This is the part that everyone overlooks! They think they need to advertise here or there. But they aren't thinking about the quality of customer they want to end up with over the course of time.

> **note** — You don't want millions of people on your list. You want 10,000 buyers who are going to be repeat purchasers on your list.

Every time you look at a website or e-zine or some other place to promote your site, you have to ask yourself if the folks who are coming to that site have an interest in eventually spending money on the things you sell. If they don't, you don't care how much traffic the salesperson for that media is telling you that he gets. It doesn't matter to you. The only thing that matters is identifying whether you're going to get the kinds of customers that you can keep for life, otherwise you've spent your ad dollars in the wrong place.

For instance, we're looking at doing a promotion that interests webmasters, search engine experts, Internet marketers, business opportunity seekers, home office workers and small businesses. Right away we get offers to advertise on "Free Lotto" and "Joke of the Day." These are great big lists on which we can advertise. Everyone starts telling me how cheap it is and how big the lists are. But that's the wrong way to think about it.

It's wrong for us because serious webmasters, business people, and search engine experts don't have the time to mess around on these sites for play and fun. People who want stuff for free and sit around the water cooler telling jokes are not the kind of business-to-business sales that I'm attempting to get in this particular campaign.

Conversely, if what you wanted were a bunch of consumers who wanted to buy travel-related products, or if you wanted consumers who wanted to buy home stereo and electronics and music, where are you going to find them? That's what you have to look at first.

> The notion of "targeting" your audience has been overused way too much. All you really have to do is think about actual people who have an interest in something. Look around on the web the same way they do. What are they going to do? Where are they going to look for your products? Where will they be when they finally see what they are looking for and buy it? Get into the minds of your target audience.

In our books we continually talk about the importance of having your display ads and banner campaigns bounce to a page that has an opt-in email list. Read this next sentence twice—you have got to collect email names, otherwise you've wasted your ad dollars.

No matter where people are coming from, you want to drive them to a page with an opt-in list. The value of your advertising is going to be based on two things:

1) What you've sold, and

2) The cost of creating your list.

Let's talk first about the value of your list. You should begin to calculate how much each name on your list is worth. For many people it is 25 cents or $1 per name. I've got a value of $3 per name on my list. That means for every person who joins my list, I know they will be worth an average of $3 each to me this year. Some recent "dot com" sales were based on $30-$40 per name. Establishing this value for your business is *very* important.

Knowing that my list is valued at $3 per name, I can run a campaign and if I get 100 people signing up for my list, then that's worth $300 to me. If out of those 100 people I get 10 sales and I make $10 per sale, that's worth another $100 to me. So the value of that campaign was worth $400 to me.

What can I afford to pay in advertising for that value? That's right. I can afford to pay $400! In other words, if I'm going to get $400 worth of value, I can only pay $400 in advertising costs.

Chapter 2

What is the best way to pay?

Now let's learn about ways to measure cost and find out how people will charge us.

CPM (cost per thousand)

Typically you'll see people charge based on CPM (cost per thousand). It's an old magazine term that has to do with the number of subscribers a magazine had and how many people would actually read it. Internet websites attempted to apply the same model, but it's really bogus. It doesn't really mean anything at all. It's not like you have subscribers looking at your magazine and getting it every month. You're just flashing a web page in front of some person. The term has much less meaning on the Internet than in traditional media where the term came from.

CPM is what the website owners want to charge you. That's their preference because it's the only thing they can really track well. It's the only thing they have control of. They can get a certain amount of traffic to their site and count how many hits or impressions they get, or better yet, the number of times a web page with your banner was displayed. Then they divide this count by 1,000 and multiply it by the CPM rate and send you a bill.

As an example, a $10/CPM rate on a site that generates 40,000 impressions would cost you $400 (That is 40,000 divided by 1,000 and multiplied by $10).

What about "branding?"

Most "ad sharks" will try to convince you that their outrageously high CPM rates are going to be important for your company's "branding." But you don't care about that. Because branding is not what most people can afford to do. As I mentioned previously, for most entrepreneurs and small to mid-sized businesses, "branding" is advertising that doesn't work.

> **note:** "Branding" is what you call your campaign when it was a total flop and you didn't sell anything and no one signed up for your email list.

All of the studies I've seen suggest that branding isn't happening on the web despite the amount of money being spent. So if anyone starts talking to you along those lines and tries to sell you CPM based advertising because of the branding value, just hang up the phone. I mean it.

The fact is, every time someone starts "selling" you on CPM based advertising and won't stop to understand what your needs are (which is building a list and making sales), then you know you've found a salesperson who just wants to hustle you and take your money.

You only want to work with the people who care about your needs as an advertiser. The kind of people who are going to give you enough value that you will want to continually advertise with them.

> **note:** The only way you're going to keep advertising is if you keep making more in value from your campaign than what it's costing you.

So in my example, I only have to be paying $200-300 dollars and getting $400 in value for me to keep placing my advertising with someone.

CPC (cost per click)

Another popular way to charge for advertising is CPC (cost per click). This is when your link or banner is on someone's page and you pay only when someone looks at it *and* clicks on it to come over to your website. This is relatively easy for programmers to track. CPC is interesting because you know you have someone actually looking at your web page, rather than just at your advertisement. You don't necessarily have someone ready to buy, but you at least have a human taking an action and getting a chance to see the first page of your sales presentation.

Chapter 2

CPC is a way for the media source and the advertiser to share in the risk. The media source hopes that it has enough "active" visitors who will be interested in the ad—and the advertiser hopes that enough of these "active" visitors will take additional action by purchasing something while on their site.

> CPC is the best type of advertising for storeowners to buy, because it ensures traffic to the site. It is also easy to verify the number of clicks that you received by looking in the log files provided by your ISP.

Calculating your cost is quite easy. You simply add the number of clicks you receive and multiply by the rate. 800 clicks that cost 50 cents each would cost $400 which would be equivalent to a $10/CPM rate on 40,000 impressions with a 2% click-through.

Some advertisers use "qualifiers" in their ads when they pay CPC. They may write something like, "My product costs more than anything else. In fact, it's $97.99 and I don't pay for shipping which is another $4.80. Click here if you are sure you want it." They don't mind paying a higher CPC rate because very few people will want the item bad enough to click on the advertising. The advertiser looks at it as getting more targeted, qualified leads and prospects.

The media source doesn't want to run ads like that because they know they are only going to send you the most qualified, cherry-picked people. They won't be making as much money on the ad. They look at this as costing money or losing revenue because they have to deliver many more impressions to break even.

CPS (cost per sale)

The advertiser will usually set up an affiliate program or revenue share program that tracks the purchases and pays a sales commission at the end of each month. This way the advertiser can quantify the cost of goods sold and can cap advertising costs at a fixed percentage of each sale. Bottom line—the advertiser only writes checks when making money.

Keep this in mind—advertisers love CPS, but the media buyers and website owners hate it. This creates a problem. It positions the media source against the advertiser. The two are at odds with each other, because they have different ideas about what they need out of the promotion.

> **note:** CPS (cost per sale) is the least risky way to buy advertising because you only pay when a sale has been made.

The media owner is now two steps away from having any control over the money he/she can make and has no control over the clicks or over the sales that are made.

> **note:** The media owner must rely on the advertiser to provide interesting ad copy or banners that will be compelling enough to get clicked on.

The advertiser is responsible for the creative end, but if "negative qualifiers" or "branding" ads are run—no one will click on them. The advertiser gets the value of the impressions while the media gets paid nothing. Believe me, they know this is not fair and they resent it.

The media owner has even less control over whether or not the advertiser's website can sell anything. All the media owner can reasonably do is get a lot of real people over to a web page. At that point it's up to the web page to make the sale. There are many reasons that the site would not make a sale:

- The order form doesn't work.

- The site is down.

- The message isn't compelling.

- The site is confusing.

- It has no defined sales process.

Chapter 2

- There's no offer, no incentive, or premium.
- The buyer is not clearly led to make a purchase.
- The ad points to a home page, not a display ad page.

All of these problems cause the prospective buyer to become confused and wander around not knowing what to do. Maybe he or she will return later, at which point the media source has lost the revenue potential of that sale. Amazon is a perfect case for this. If the shopper bookmarks the Amazon.com page and comes back later, the media source will never receive any benefit for bringing eyeballs there and introducing them to Amazon.

> **note** People place advertisements for Amazon, but they only get paid when the person buys that book immediately.

Playing with the big boys

Currently, a lot of the bigger, higher traffic sites are not doing any revenue share or affiliate programs. They won't even talk to you about CPS advertising. A lot of the web sites that are venture capital funded, and are getting all their revenue from advertising, only care about CPM impression-based advertising. They only care about their own ad sales and monetizing their own traffic. These web sites don't care about you as an advertiser, and they hire very slick salesmen to hustle you into spending way more in advertising than you will ever see a return on. Be forewarned!

When you start calling around to the ad networks like DoubleClick, FlyCast, or 24/7, you will get to meet people who are in the business of brokering advertising. They don't really care about the media source or the advertiser. All they care about is getting enough money in the pipeline and moving dollars back and forth into their pocket. In fact, someone said that the Internet has created a huge funnel of money coming out of venture capitalists' pockets and going into the hands of ad agencies and banner networks. It's a

33

sad state of affairs. None of this money floating around is creating a real sale or benefit.

What can a poor boy do?

Step-by-step strategy

As a first time advertiser, or small- to medium-sized business, you can't afford to play these games. So what do you do? Here are my strategies:

Step One—Think like your customers

I determine where my prospects go, what keywords they use, and which websites they are likely to find.

The first thing you have to do is examine the places where interested people go when they come on the Internet. The way you do that is to turn on your browser and click on What's New, What's Cool, and the search box. When your prospects do a search, what words do they put in? Where do they end up?

I use Super-Seek.com to investigate what's on the search engines. It pulls up all the search engines right away so I can instantly see what consumers are presented with. If I were a consumer interested in a particular product, how would I know where to find it? Maybe I would type in a search, but maybe the product I'm looking for is on a main directory listing.

Your job is to look in the directory listings and use the search engines to find the web pages that pop up. These are the most obvious and immediate places where people who have a real interest in your product are going to end up. Isn't that where you want to have your advertising placed? Think about it.

Of course, this requires time and effort. You have to care about it. But the fact is, this exercise will save you thousands in advertising costs. No one else is going to care about your money as you do.

Step Two—Know who you are dealing with

When I have identified several easy-to-find websites, I take a hard look at them and try to determine the owner's degree of sophistication.

What are the interests of this web site owner? Was this page put up because it was a work of passion or a hobby? Or because of hopes to hit the billion dollar dream? Is there a lot of venture capital money behind the owner and now the site must sell advertising? Was it put it up because as a small business it is trying to sell its own product? Does the site hope to make a little bit of money by joining affiliate programs and selling a little advertising? Ask these questions as you look at the site.

When you look at the web page you have to think. Get an assessment of the individual, the real human. When you look at the web page, you have to act as though you're sitting across the negotiating table from the other person. Or as though you're getting ready to play poker with a stranger.

> **note** If you have a limited budget, you really want to focus on the sites that aren't as concerned about hustling you for ad dollars. There are a lot of them. And a lot of those sites have really good, qualified traffic.

Here's the deal—if you're getting ready to play poker with one of your buddies, you have a whole different attitude than if you were getting ready to play poker with card sharks in Las Vegas. One of them is sitting there ready to take your money. That's all he or she cares about. The other one wants to hang out and spend time with you. Do you see what I mean?

We want to pay the bare minimum to place our ad and links to our website on as many other websites as possible. We try to make a determination of how *little* we have to spend by carefully analyzing sites before contacting them.

Step Three—Negotiate ruthlessly!

Follow this train of thought and learn the secrets for getting *free* and low-cost advertising. Here's what I do:

If there is absolutely no advertising on the site and it's just a lot of great free information, I'll email the owner and praise him/her for the great information and articles. Then I ask him/her if he would like to have more informational content, articles, and other things of interest for his readers, to add to his page. I *do not* ask him to join my affiliate program or talk to him about advertising. I *do not* ask him about his ad rates or tell him to send me his media kit. He won't know what I'm talking about. And he probably hates advertisers. He probably doesn't want advertising on his page—that's why there isn't any on it.

The other thing I look for is a page that has a bunch of links on it. You'll find lots of these on top of the search engines. I email these folks and talk to them about adding my link to their page—*not* trading links—just adding mine to their page. They've already shown me that they're happy to do that. They have put up links to other people. I make suggestions about why they would like to put up my link first. I provide some copy and tell them about my site, suggesting it would look good on their site as a benefit for the people coming to their resource page.

If I get a response back and he says yes, great. If I don't get a response back in a few days, I will contact them asking if they had a chance to look at my page and if they plan to add a link to it or not. I'll mention that I was considering putting up a link on my page to promote their site because I like it so much. If they put up a link then I put up a link for them and everything's great. If not, I wait a couple more days. Then I put up their link and tell them to take a look at it. I ask if they would please do me a favor and add a link on their page for the trade we've been talking about.

Offer something worth MORE than money!

If that doesn't work, I go to the next level of negotiation, assuming this is a page that is prominent on the search engines and a place I want to be seen. If that is the case, I offer to trade them something for the advertising. See if you can find out what their interests are. Then look at the products that you sell. I might say "As a 'Thank You' for putting up my link, I'd like to send you the latest CD from my store from the artist of your choice. I'd like to give you that as a free gift, my way of saying thank you for putting up a link."

You could offer to pay them—but most people who are into trading and sharing links don't know how to value paid advertising. Money doesn't mean anything to them. That's not why they have a website! If you offer to give them something in exchange, such as promoting their site, or give them something they might really like, it means much more (especially if you could mail it to them). If you just mail them a check, it's like "whatever...I made a little money off my site." But if you mailed them something from your store or some product that was inexpensive, they would talk about you and show it to everyone they know. They would love to promote your link.

You can establish relationships with people that will be more valuable than anything—just by sending them some of your product. We did this with a CD cleaner. What did we do? We said "We would like you to try this new product. Why don't you take a look at it?" The next thing we knew, they had placed big banners right across the top of their pages. They even made banners for us! They placed feature presentations right in the middle of their home page. They put links to us from their navigation buttons on the side strip, with little stars next to it. They added personal comments and said "This is great. check it out!" They did all of this for us because they were so enthused and excited that we actually sent them something for free in the mail. Believe me, this is powerful marketing!

Here's a summary of low cost ad strategies

These are the first few strategies. Notice how I'm working up the food chain. Start with articles. Trade if you have to. Then give them something if you have to. And as a last resort—pay them—but only if you really have to.

These types of promotion strategies are extremely important because:

- They are very low cost.

- They don't take up much of your time.

- Those links will stay there forever.

Pay attention to that last point. These links will never be taken down. It's the most long ranging campaign that you can do. You'll have benefits months and months after you put up those links.

What's up with banners?

Banners are an easy thing for webmasters to put on their pages. You must learn to analyze the particular type of banners that are displayed. Here's why—the type of banners on a site will immediately tell you how sophisticated the media owner is. This is a pivotal point in how you approach your negotiations.

Ask yourself these questions:

- Are they "link exchange" banners, where they are trying to promote their site through cross promotion?

- Are these "affiliate program" banners, where they are hoping to make a small commission on sales?

- Are these banners for paid advertisers?

Chapter 2

Link exchange banners

If the banners are there for link exchange types of places, then you know that what is important to this person is to promote his or her site. That's why the banner was put up—to get a little promotion. LinkExchange.com is the most prominent of the bunch, but if you want to see an alphabetical listing of all free banner exchanges in the known universe, check out:

http://www.bxmegalist.com/A-to-Z.htm

When I write to a person who has these types of banners, I explain that I'd like to do something for him or her, maybe trade them a little tit for tat. I suggest we could do some promoting for each other. I tell them about the kind of traffic that comes to my site. I mention that I was thinking about putting his or her site on my link page and that he/she might do the same thing for me.

Maybe I could write a little article for him or her, or maybe I could put up a little page that endorses him or her and refers people to his or her site. I ask if I could do something for him or her on my site and see if he or she could do something for me on his or her site. I always end with, "It occurs to me that we've got similar customers interested in us, but we both have non-competing products. We're not competitors at all, and people who buy from me would love to come over and see your page. So what can we do together? Shall we exchange banners?"

You would personally exchange banners with people with whom you want to network. These people are going to be advertising for you for free. They will have links back to your page. Since they understand what link exchange banners are, I also try to get them to put up a special page or something on their home page. Then I put up a special page on my site and write a custom blurb about these folks. Not only will these pages stay there forever, but now you've created a true relationship with someone that will pay off in dividends for years to come.

39

Affiliate program banners

The next thing to determine is whether they've joined an affiliate program. You can usually tell by the banners because the URL contains questions marks, numbers and codes, and maybe the name of their site. You can recognize these after awhile. The best resource directory for these programs can be found at:

http://www.associateprograms.com/

If you've read Declan Dunn's book *Winning the Affiliate Game*, you'll really begin to understand the power of affiliate programs. So do the people who display these banners. They realize that by simply joining an affiliate program, they can make a little ad revenue without having to "sell" advertising. This is better than putting up a banner that's just trading traffic. With an affiliate banner they get paid on every sale.

If someone has put up those types of banners, it tells you that he or she understands what affiliate programs are all about—having demonstrated a willingness to get paid on a per sale basis. As I mentioned earlier, this is the most favorable situation for you, the advertiser!

It is *so easy* to work with these people! All you do is look at which programs they've joined, then go see how much those merchants are paying in percentages. Simply offer them one or two percent more on your product than what they are getting currently on the programs they've already joined.

> **note** You don't want CPM or CPC. What you really want is CPS, *cost per sale*, and the people who put up affiliate banners have already told you by their actions that they are more than happy to take cost per sale.

This is not hard because most of the programs that they've joined are paying at the most a meager 5-12%. If you have your own products to sell you can really clean up. Especially if you are high on the food chain, like a manufacturer or distributor. Even retailers who get 50% keystone margins can afford to pay out 10-12% for a guaranteed sale. We usually give our affiliates 25%. Many retailers also give 25%, especially if they have 50% profit in an item. They don't mind giving up half, because it makes sense. They are simply splitting the profits with someone who will make the sales for them.

That leads to one other powerful idea. Joint ventures. If you have found a sales strategy that works then offer to split your profits with someone in exchange for an endorsed mailing to their opt-in list. The idea is simple. You set up the process and write the email sales letter. Your joint venture partner puts his or her name on the letter and emails it to everyone as though it came from them. This can be a great way to test—but it can also be quite expensive since you are giving away half of your profit! As soon as your process is proven to work, then take the gamble and pay money for your advertising. You will make a *lot* more in the long run.

Paid advertising banners

Finally, let's take a look at people who have paid advertising banners on their site. You know one thing—someone is giving them money. You will have to pay them money also. The amount you have to pay will be in direct proportion to how much they have already been offered. How simple this is.

These guys are a little more sophisticated and they've been around long enough that they are probably good at hustling and "selling" their space to advertisers. Watch out!

> **note** Paid advertising is extremely worthwhile, especially if the media source cares about your needs as an advertiser.

Take a look at the banner ads other people are running, sorted by keyword:

http://www.namestake.com/

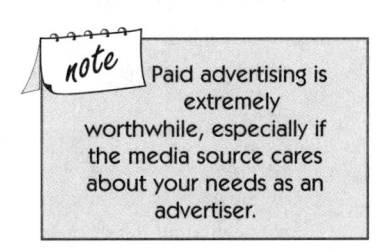

41

We try to make deals with them on a cost per-sale or cost per-click basis. The first thing we do is send a short, to-the-point email. In the subject line it says "We would like to advertise on your site." Or it says "What are your ad rates?" There's no mystery here about what this email is about. If they accept paid advertising on their website they are going to read this email.

Then we tell them we're interested in placing a banner on their site, or we're interested in placing a text link, or we're interested in partnering with them through our affiliate program. Just be specific. Explain whatever your deal is so they can understand what you want them to do.

Then tell them what you pay on a per click basis. Try to stay in the 10-25 cent range depending on what your qualifier is. This may depend on how much traffic they get. Or you might start out with a different rate for a limited test run. Try to present them with a range or sliding scale of what you are willing to pay.

What you really want is a response from them. Keep them curious. Keep things open-ended so they have to get back to you to start the negotiations. Tell them your high and low for per-click deals and your proposed percentage on a per-sale basis. Ask them if your offer is interesting to them. Ask leading questions that beg for an answer. What are their ad rates? Do they have a media kit? Can they provide you with demographics? How long have they been advertising? How much traffic does their site get? The only point of sending out this email is to get a response. If they answer you, then you have the opportunity to start negotiating.

At the end of the email I always write, "We do business with people who call us and talk to us about how we can advertise together. Here's my number. Call me directly. Call me collect if you have to." I do this because email is lousy for negotiating! If I don't get them on the phone, I can't figure out what their bargaining points are. I can't go back and forth with them while working out the best deal. If I can't talk to them, I can't negotiate effectively.

Chapter 2

A lot of people want to use email for negotiating, but email is about as effective as using telegrams to put together a deal. It can't be done well. There's not enough back and forth, not enough interaction. You can't tell voice inflection. You can't tell humor. You can't warm up or bond with people with telegrams or email. You must make it a priority to get them on the phone with you.

If they call you back and start hustling you on CPM, thank them politely and say you're sorry but your policy is only to pay on a per-click or per-sale basis. Then ask which one they are most interested in! If it's neither one, then say "In that case, if you really want to sell the CPM, then what I propose is a two day test. That way we can both track the impressions from your site to make sure our systems report the same information." This two-day test will tell you everything you need to know about the value of this website's advertising potential to your bottom line. Simply count the number of additional clicks or hits to your page in those two days, then add up the number of extra sales. From that, you decide whether you can afford to pay for their traffic or not.

Read this twice!

Identify where you want to place your ads, then analyze the different types of site owners and learn how to approach each one in the least costly way—that's the lesson. If you didn't catch on to this, then you should re-read this entire article.

People who approach everyone with the same message will get fewer links than you and will pay way more in advertising costs. Now that you are tuned in, you will be able to get the best placement at the lowest cost every single time.

There you have it. These strategies have never before been revealed. Now you know the secrets that have been the driving force behind the national campaigns that ADNet International has been involved with over the years.

Banner advertising (per-impression and per-click)

Banner advertising is probably one of the least-effective forms of advertising, but it still has its uses. Before you start purchasing massive banner advertising, be sure you know what your conversion rate and cost/revenue per visitor is—that's the only way you can know what banner advertising rates will work for you.

Let me illustrate:

Say you did a test of 2000 impressions (meaning 2000 people SAW your banner on a web page), and of those 2000 impressions, you got 100 visitors to your site. Furthermore, of those 100 visitors, say you got 1 sale. For this example, let's say your average sale amount is $100 with the profit being $50.

Here are some simple numbers you could generate from this test:

Click Conversion Ratio: 100/2000 = 0.005 = 0.5%

Profit per 1000 impressions: $25

So this simple (and many would say not statistically valid because of the relatively low number of impressions) test tells you that you can afford to pay $25 per thousand (CPM) for your banner advertising. That's a "break-even" number. Some people are happy to break even on the front end, relying on "back-end" sales to make their profit. If you wanted to actually make money on the "front end," you'd need to find banner advertising at rates less than $25 CPM.

I've seen CPM rates as low as $2, but that's "run of network," meaning your banners would be shown to everyone, not just people visiting sites related to your product/service—your conversion rate would be drastically reduced in this kind of arrangement.

Chapter 2

Don't think a single test of 2000 impressions can be extrapolated to infinity—you will need to be tracking and evaluating your ad results continually. If you get lazy and stop doing this, you'll be running blind, never knowing if your ad dollars are increasing or decreasing your bottom line.

> **note** You should be able to find "targeted" banner advertising for $10-15 CPM.

An inexpensive and risk-free way to test your banners is to use one of these banner exchange services:

BannersGoMLM: http://www.bannersgomlm.com

LinkExchange/bCentral: http://adnetwork.bcentral.com

GSA: http://einets.com/stats/gsa

LookSmart: http://www.looksmartclicks.com

TrafficTool: http://www.traffictool.com/cgi-bin/index.cgi

These companies allow you to place their banner on your various web pages. Anytime someone views their banner on your page, you get an impression "credit." Usually you exchange at a 2:1 ratio, so for every 2 impressions of their banner on your site, you get 1 impression of your banner on someone else's site (some exchange rates are better than this though).

These banner exchanges also have some fairly useful banner creation utilities they encourage you to use free of charge, as often as you need.

The banner you're using will have a significant effect on your click-through ratio. For some great tips on banner design, check out this site:

BannerTips: http://www.bannertips.com

45

Also, you can have your banners designed for you by a number of companies. The two resources below will design your banners and Scott Covert will even guarantee a click-through ratio significantly higher than the industry average:

BannerWorkz: http://www.bannerworkz.com

Scott Covert: http://www.successinformation.com/banners.htm

Okay, once you have a good tested banner with tested conversion rates, here are a number of companies you can purchase banner advertising through. One of my favorites is "AdFlight"—they allow you to bid on "remnant" space and I've seen some pretty good deals available there.

Some of these companies offer "pay per click" advertising as well, but as Patrick pointed out in the above article, they're mostly pushing the "CPM" (cost per 1000 impressions) service.

Burst:	http://www.burstmedia.com/release/advertisers/advertiser.asp
Ad Flight:	http://www.adflight.com
Penny Web:	http://www.pennyweb.com
FlyCast:	http://www.flycast.com/advertisers
DoubleClick:	http://www.doubleclick.com
L90:	http://www.l90.net
ValueClick:	http://valueclick.com
24/7 Media:	http://www.247media.com
Phase2:	http://www.phase2media.com

Chapter 2

VantageNet:	http://apps3.vantagenet.com/site/adacct.asp
Save-Audit:	http://www.safe-audit.com/advertisers_index.html
Aaddzz:	http://www.aaddzz.com
B-Central:	http://www.bcentral.com
Auction.com:	http://www.biddersedge.com/advertising.jsp
BannerPool:	http://www.bannerpool.com

Pay-per-click search engines

Pay-Per-Click search engines are relatively new, and have been causing quite a stir in the small-business Internet marketing circles. They are also one of the most effective ways to get targeted traffic to your site.

To the person looking for information about a specific topic, these search engines appear to work like any of the others. The difference is the listings are purchased by the advertisers—the highest bidding advertiser for the keyword "candy" is listed at the top of the page when someone does a search for that word. The advertiser with the next-highest bid gets the 2nd spot, and so on.

Jim Daniels wrote an article about how to best use "GoTo.com" (the 1st and most popular of the pay-per-click search engines)—for the most part, his methods will work for the others too. The article is followed by a few more resources related to pay-per-click search engines.

"Traffic For Pennies...."

By Jim Daniels

What follows is a proven, step by step formula for driving highly targeted traffic to any website—for pennies.

47

> **note** In a nutshell, GoTo.com is a "pay for rank" search engine. It allows website owners to bid on keywords related to their site.

Recently, I've been sampling new promotional methods to drive fresh traffic to my website. I had been reading quite a bit about GoTo.com and how other webmasters had been getting great results with it, so I decided to give it a try.

When users search on any term at GoTo.com they are presented with a list of sites, with the highest bidders appearing closest to the top.

Based upon my own experience, this site not only offers a great way to find things on the web, it offers a very inexpensive way to generate targeted traffic to any site. By following the details of my own GoTo advertising campaign, you should be able to emulate the excellent results I've had.

Just a few weeks into my campaign, I am now generating between 85 and 100 visitors each day from GoTo.com. My costs are averaging about 4 bucks a day. As I continue to tweak my advertising (I'll teach you how) I expect my numbers to double and possibly triple. But I'll get to that in a minute. Let's take things a step at a time.

Step 1: Open your own GoTo account.

The first step is to visit www.GoTo.com and open an account. There is a minimum investment of $25 to become a GoTo advertiser. The way it works is simple. As an advertiser at GoTo.com, you bid on search terms relevant to your site. You have complete control over how much you pay on a per-click basis on each of those search terms. The higher your "bid" on each search term, the higher in the search results your site will appear. As Goto proudly states, "It's targeted, cost-per-click advertising and you set the cost per click."

Step 2: Decide how much a visitor is worth to you.

You can do this by checking your current website stats. Add up your average number of monthly visitors and determine what percentage of them actually go on to become a customer. This can be tricky but it is an important step. Depending upon the average cost of your products or services, you should be able to come up with a ballpark figure as to what each visitor is worth.

Example: If I'm converting one sale from every 100 visitors and my average sale is $100, then each visitor is worth about a buck. (Keep in mind, this does not take into account the lifetime value of a site visitor or customer.)

Once you have an idea of how much each visitor is worth to you, write it down. You will use this number as a "cap" on your bids. More about this later.

Step 3: Start a file on your computer with keywords pertaining to your site.

Using any word processor, start typing anything and everything you can think of that pertains to your site. If you are selling pet supplies your list would look something like this:

- dog
- cat
- kitten
- dog bone
- collar
- dog food
- pet
- pet supply

(Don't worry about pluralizing all your words. GoTo's Search Pluralization feature analyzes your keywords and does this for you automatically.)

> **note** A large list allows you to bid as low as a penny on 90% of your keywords. Even if 10% of them get a single click each day, you're generating 100 visitors right there.

Now before you tackle this step, I must inform you that this can be the most time-consuming part of your GoTo campaign. Why? Well, in order to really get the most from your campaign you'll be making a list of at least 1000 keywords, or search terms. That's right, I said one thousand. You don't "need" that many to get started with GoTo, but I tried bidding on a limited number of keywords and the results were nowhere near the cost-effectiveness of using a large list.

GoTo offers a "suggested search terms tool" to help you:

http://inventory.GoTo.com/inventory/searchInventory.mp

When you type in a word there, you get a list of related search terms that were searched on last month at GoTo.com. I found their suggestion tool helpful, although it can still take quite a bit of time to compile a large list with it.

Actually, I must admit I cheated on generating my own keyword list. As a registered member of The Challenge, I have access to a keyword generation script that generated literally 1200 terms for me in a few minutes. This tool saved me days of thinking and typing and quite frankly is worth the price of admission to the private site. (Especially if you are planning a GoTo campaign.)

Step 4: Write a title and description to go along with your keywords.

When you place your bids at GoTo.com you will also be asked for the title of the URL you are submitting and a short description. It is important to write something brief, yet eye-catching.

> **note** Remember, the main objective is to get people to click. Use of the words "free" and "you" can be very useful here.

Stick to the tried and true classified advertising axioms, but make an effort to stand out from the crowd. A good idea is to write something *you* would click on.

You may want to write two or three of these titles and descriptions, especially if you plan to bid on keywords that cannot be directed to the exact same URL at your site. Example: One of my bids was on the keywords "free downloads" so I wrote a separate title and description for the software area of my site, http://bizweb2000.com/software.htm and submitted that specific URL.

You can save time if you can write a description that covers your entire site and then link all your bids to your main URL. Although your traffic may not be as targeted when you do this, it is less time consuming than trying to break your site into specific areas. It all depends on your individual site and how much time you have to spend. (Remember, you can always adjust links once your account is online and drawing traffic.)

Step 5: Place your bids.

Okay, you have a nice long list of keywords, along with titles and descriptions. Now it's time to get your bids in! You do this at GoTo's DirecTraffic Center. This is their account management tool, where you can add, modify, or delete your search listings, 24 hours/day, 7 days/week. You can also check your account balance, add money to your GoTo account, change your bids in real-time and view your activity reports. Once you've opened an account you just click http://secure.GoTo.com/s/dtc/center/ to log in.

As far as actually placing your bids, there are basically two methods to utilize—manually (by hand) or by using the Excel spreadsheet they offer. This is a no-brainer. Go for the faster and more accurate spreadsheet option. It allows you to complete one form and email it to chgorder@GoTo.com for their review.

Microsoft's™ Excel is part of the Office Suite and many PC users have it, even though they may never use it. Although I had never opened Microsoft's™ Excel program before, I was able to learn enough in about a half hour to get me through. Basic skills like repeating text and drag and drop of my keyword list were simple enough to figure out. Within an hour of downloading the spreadsheet they offer, I had a completed form ready with over 1200 keyword bids.

An important topic to touch on here is the pricing of your bids. Since you will undoubtedly be submitting some keywords that are not currently being bid on at GoTo, why pay more

> **note** I suggest you price all your bids at one cent (0.01).

per click than you have to? A penny bid will put you at the top on these keywords! Once your spreadsheet has been accepted and put online, you can then start adjusting for more traffic. (More on this in the next step.)

Make sure your spreadsheet does not contain off-topic keywords. Submissions are spot-checked and routinely refused if they contain keywords unrelated to your site.

Step 6: Adjust your bids.

This is where knowing what a click is worth to you comes into play. At Goto.com's DirecTraffic Center you can now adjust your bids in real-time. This area shows you your current ranking on each of the terms you've bid on and also tells you how much you need to bid to get to the #1 spot. What a tool!

While I don't recommend you go for number one with every bid I do recommend you try for a top 50 spot. As of the writing of this, each page returned on GoTo searches returns 40 sites. Getting your keywords on the first page or even the very top of the second can generate traffic.

What has been working for me is this: As I go through my bids I only adjust the ones that I feel are highly likely to get searched for. If I can squeeze into the top ten on any of these by adding a few cents to the bid, I do it. Then, I make sure that the real common and super-busy keywords appear at least in the top 50.

Example: The word "business" was very popular and my penny bid had me at #153. I had received zero hits from that low position. So I bid just enough to move it up to the top 50 spot and bingo—six hits the next day. While you may be thinking that six hits is nothing, remember that I'm bidding on 1200 keywords. I've had time to adjust about 35% of them so far and I'm up to 100 visitors a day from GoTo.com. That's over 3000 visitors a month and I'm far from done.

As I mentioned, knowing what a click is worth to you comes in handy here. If each visitor to your site is worth say, .65, then set that as your limit, or cap. Bid up to that amount on any keyword, but not over it. This will ensure that your campaign remains profitable.

As you make adjustments to your bids, you should visit the "view stats" area of the DirecTraffic Center frequently. Checking your stats at least once each week will allow you to keep on top of your adjustments and maximize your traffic.

That's it. An effective new traffic source for your site.

In closing

While I'm not much for spending money on advertising, this new method is cheap and effective. Anytime you can get targeted traffic to your site for pennies, you need to take action.

I've managed to get some excellent results with GoTo.com, even with the huge amount of competition in my industry. For other webmasters who are focused on less crowded niches, GoTo.com could be a goldmine of targeted business.

Take this lesson plan and GoTo it!

This article was written by Jim Daniels of JDD Publishing. Jim's site has helped 1000's of regular folks profit online. Visit http://bizweb2000.com for free "how-to" cybermarketing assistance, software, manuals, web services and more. No time to visit the site? Subscribe to their free, weekly *BizWeb E-Gazette:* mailto:freegazette@bizweb2000.com

Allan Gardyne, primarily known as the "affiliate program guy" (more on that later) also runs one of the best sites about pay-per-click search engines:

> http://www.payperclicksearchengines.com

At last count, he had 34 search engines listed there, along with several resources and articles related to using them.

Three of the best known pay-per-click search engines are:

1) http://www.GoTo.com

2) http://www.kanoodle.com

3) http://www.bay9.com (formerly rocketlinks.com)

Again, GoTo.com is by far the most used of any of these.

> **note** One crucial element of your pay-per-click search engine work is the keywords you are gunning for.

Obviously if you have an online jewelry store, you want your site to come up when someone searches for "jewelry." However, your site conversion rate may not justify paying the per-click rate necessary to get a "top-10" position at GoTo.com.

Chapter 2

So you need to come up with other words which are:

- related to your business
- actually being used by people on the pay-per-click search engines

For instance, you could try these words individually and in combination with each other: "ring," "diamond," "necklace," "wedding band," "bracelet," "earring," etc.

As you might expect, a number of tools have popped up to aid you in your keyword selection. Here are a couple:

http://www.wordtracker.com

http://www.jimtools.com/keywords.html

Use the following resources to find top keywords and phrases people type into search engines:

http://50.lycos.com

http://www.wordspot.com

http://www.analogx.com/cgi-bin/keytally.exe

http://searchenginewatch.com/facts/searches.html

http://inventory.GoTo.com/inventory/Search_Suggestion.jhtml

Be sure to check out this little gem—it's a free piece of software that queries GoTo and other search engines to see what users search for.

http://www.goodkeywords.com

I also ran across a nifty tool to help you with your "Goto.com" listings—anyone serious about using pay-per-click search engines (and anyone concerned with getting targeted traffic should be) will save hours of time with this tool:

http://www.paidsearchenginetools.com

Pay-per-action advertising

With pay-per-action advertising, the advertiser only pays money when a prospect takes some specific action. Such actions might include:

- filling out a registration form
- submitting an application
- requesting more information
- downloading a specific file

The beauty of pay-per-action advertising is you are really paying for leads now, rather than traffic. If someone takes the time to submit a form, they're showing a definite interest in what you have to offer.

I've seen a lot of programs paying $0.50 to $2.00 per "action"—if you can convert even a minimal number of those leads to sales, you'll be "in the money."

Here are a few of the companies that offer per-action advertising (some of them refer to it as "per-lead" advertising):

http://www.safe-audit.com/advertisers_index.html

http://www.cj.com

http://www.clickxchange.com

http://www.onresponse.com

http://www.websponsors.com

http://www.directleads.com

Ezine advertising

I'm talking about advertising in electronic magazines (Ezines) other than your own here. (I discuss having your own Ezine in the "Ezine" section).

The most significant factor is the audience served by the Ezine in question. Don't advertise women's cosmetics in an Ezine devoted to men's soccer. I believe the next most significant factors are the number of ads in the publication and the placement of your ad. Ads generally pull best in the following order:

note: Ezine advertising can be very effective if done right. What do I mean by "done right"?

1) exclusive mailing

2) ads at the top of an Ezine with few ads

3) ads at the bottom of an Ezine with few ads

4) ads in the middle of an Ezine with few ads

5) ads in an Ezine with many other ads

Exclusive mailings mean your ad is the only thing sent to the recipient. While these are the most effective, they're also the most expensive. Be sure you've done some of the less expensive advertising in the same Ezine (with good results!) before you commit to a $2,000 exclusive ad.

I would be remiss if I didn't mention this: If you know of a very good Ezine related to your product/service, and your advertising funds are low, you should definitely attempt to arrange a joint venture (see the section on Joint Ventures) with the owner. You may pay more per sale this way than if you just advertised, but you have absolutely zero risk.

Here are a few resources where you can probably find dozens of Ezines related to your product or service. Some of them even include an advertising service that will save you lots of time.

http://www.lifestylespub.com

http://www.liszt.com

http://www.topezineads.com

http://www.e-zinez.com

http://www.opt-influence.com

http://www.e-target.com

Opt-in email advertising

note: Opt-in email advertising is the practice of sending out emails to people who have never heard of you or your company, and have never interacted with you in any way—or have asked you to remove them from your email list.

This is a perfect time to bring up the topic of SPAM and/or "Unsolicited Commercial Email (UCE)" and/or "Bulk E-mail."

My recommendation is simple: don't do it. If you send out unsolicited emails, you will very likely lose your Internet access—and you could also quite possibly find yourself facing civil and criminal charges.

Chapter 2

Now, "Opt-in" email is different. With opt-in email, the people on the list have theoretically "opted in". They have said, "Sure, I'd like to hear from people offering products/services related to _____." (Fill in the blank with some topic.)

I say *theoretically* because unless *you* are the one securing these sign ups, you can only rely on the word of the opt-in company. Be sure to quiz them on the exact methods used to obtain the email addresses. If you're not comfortable they are truly "opt-in," then walk away.

Just like traditional (through the mail) direct marketing, the best list to sell to is your own "in-house" list. In fact, some people have made their fortune giving away a "front end" product just to build their own list—and then they promote to that list ceaselessly.

If you don't have your own list yet, or you just want to expand your reach, there are a number of companies that offer mailing services to "opt-in" lists. In every case they will do the mailing to the list (this is to prevent unethical advertisers from abusing the list). The mailing usually costs 15-25 cents per name. So on a mailing to 2000 people, you'd need a gross profit of $150-250 to "break even." Like everything else, this method of marketing requires testing.

Here are a few providers of mailing services to "opt-in" lists:

http://www.matchlogic.com/services/acquisition_marketing/delivere.asp

http://www.digitalworks.com/onlinead/directemail

http://www.Postmasterdirect.com

http://www.optininc.com

http://www.permissiondirect.com

http://www.2sendit.com

http://edirect.com

http://www.datandomains.com/leads

Press releases

I'm not going to pretend to be an expert on press releases, as I haven't made much use of them personally—much to my detriment, I'm sure. However, once I get this book finished, I'm going to give it a go.

There's lots of information about how to write a press release (there are specific requirements) which will not only get published, but will result in tons of calls, requests for interviews, and if you play your cards right, an avalanche of new business.

> **note** A well-written press release can be more beneficial to your business than thousands of dollars of paid advertising.

Here are a few:

http://www.xpresspress.com/PRnotes.html

http://www.netdummy.com/archives/022200.html#how

http://www.pressflash.com/anatomy.html

http://www.netpress.org/careandfeeding.html

http://www.dern.com/welltemp.html

http://www.smithfam.com/news/a10.html

http://www.prprofits.com/killer.html

Chapter 2

Here's a very useful guide for writing for the press:

http://www.communications.uci.edu/style/style1.html

As you might imagine, there are a number of companies offering press release creation and distribution services:

http://usanews.net

http://www.PRweb.com

http://www.urlwire.com

http://www.netpost.com

http://www.newswire.com

http://www.newsbureau.com

http://www.prnewswire.com

http://www.pressflash.com

http://www.xpresspress.com

http://www.businesswire.com

http://www.press-releases.net

http://www.m2.com/M2_PressWIRE/index.html

http://www.comitatusgroup.com/pr/index.htm

http://www.imediafax.com
(Select media and fax online—0.25¢ page faxed)

http://www.digitalwork.com/publicrel/sendpr/

61

http://www.drnunley.com/release.htm
(Dr. Nunley will write and send out to 5000 media contacts for $175)

There's also a fair amount of software designed to help you send out your own press releases:

ABC Press Release: http://www.abcreports.com/PressRelease

Press Submitter: http://www.sharpspider.com/press

PR Wizard: http://www.prwizard.com

Media Magnet: http://www.media-magnet.com

Press Hound: http://www.presshound.com

News Pro: http://www.news-pro.com

Press Blaster: http://www.pressblaster.net

JOC Press Release: http://www.jocsoft.com

Press Manager: http://accessarts.net/store/pressfaq.shtml

In looking at the list of features/benefits for these packages, it looks like some of them may be private-labeled versions of "Media Magnet." I know this is true with "Press Hound" and "Press Manager," and suspect it may be true with some of the others as well.

Article submission / distribution

One of the most effective ways of advertising is to write articles and then submit those articles to various online publications. A perfect example of this is Jim Daniels' article, which I reprinted in this guide (see the section on pay-per-click search engines).

Chapter 2

Jim could (and probably did) submit that article to various online publications. Some of them would probably publish it, and a fair number of that publication's readers would click on at least one of the links to Jim's web site in that article.

Did you notice the "resource info and link" at the end of Jim's article? One of these should be included in every article you submit for publication—otherwise it just doesn't do you much good to have your article in circulation.

Rick Beneteau has written a book about this method of advertising—it's quite reasonably priced and a great resource for anyone who wants to advertise in this manner.

http://www.ezineMoney.net

If you don't want to write your own articles, Dr. Nunley will write and submit your article to various (relevant) publications. I was surprised at the low cost of this service!

http://www.drnunley.com/COPY.htm

(You specify the topic and approve the article before he sends it out.)

If you're a prolific writer, there's a great way for you to make your articles available to web site owners automatically. The web site owner simply pastes two lines of JavaScript code on their web pages, and your article (updated automatically whenever you change the "master" copy of the article) appears at that location on their web page. The software is called *Master Syndicator* and can be found at this location:

http://mastersyndicator.com

63

Sweepstakes / contests

Magazines have been using sweepstakes for years, and they can work for your business too. There are some legal considerations to be aware of though, especially if a purchase is required for entry.

I decided to put this in at the last minute, so I only have a couple of related links for you to check out. I'll add more links to the directory in the members section of my website as soon as I get them. In fact, I'll probably create a simple program that will allow you to administer your own sweepstakes with minimal effort (I couldn't find any sweepstakes software out there—unbelievable). "How to," legal considerations, and lots more information can be found here:

> http://sweepstakes.doubleclick.net/help

Sweepstakes Service: http://sweepstakes.doubleclick.net

Miscellaneous advertising / promotion resources

These resources are too broad in scope for the above categories, but contain lots of solid information, tools, and services to aid you in your advertising and promotion efforts:

Web Sites:

> http://www.virtualpromote.com

> http://www.drnunley.com/

> http://www.wilsonweb.com

Chapter 2

http://www.thewritemarket.com/mcnn

[Marketing Course Newsletter Network "Ultimate Marketing Guide"]

Ezine Ads/Banner Ads/Transfer Ads—low prices, huge quantities:

Quality? Better test before you bet the farm!

http://rankyou.com/promo/

Software tools for promotion implementation, tracking, and management:

http://www.swissarmyapp.com

http://www.roibot.com

Affiliate programs

3

Affiliate programs

I'm going to start this topic with an excerpt from Declan Dunn's book, *The Complete Insider's Guide to Associate and Affiliate Programs*. Declan is one of the top affiliate program consultants, and I count myself very fortunate to be working with him at ADNet.

If you're not familiar with affiliate programs, this will be a great introduction to their potential benefits to you as a business owner. If you already have a good understanding of affiliate programs and how you can use them in your own business, you may skip this article and get right to the resources.

What affiliate programs are and how to put them to use for you

by Declan Dunn

Excerpted from "The Complete Insider's Guide to Associate and Affiliate Programs" (http://activemarketplace.com/w.cgi?insiders-1306 – affiliate link)

Affiliate Program: Targeting a customer base and the web sites most frequently visited, a business sets up an Internet sales system that moves the consumer from visiting another site to a point of sale at its web site.

> Sometimes called an *affiliate* or *associate program, resellers, revenue sharing programs, per inquiry/per clickthrough sales*, or *per sales commissions*, the online affiliate programs simply make it easy for your customer to find you through high traffic, niche sites on the Internet. In exchange for forwarding you customers, the web site owner/affiliate is rewarded each time one of their consumers makes a purchase at your site.

In this book you will learn how to quickly set up your own affiliate program. You will be able to:

- Precisely describe your customer profile in terms of demographics, interests, and the places on the Internet your customers visit.

- Develop a sales system that invites customers to visit your web site and rewards the affiliate with a commission per lead or per sale.

- Test your system and automate the sales process that makes the purchase decision easy, and follows up with customers who often do not buy on first contact.

- Convert a significant number of visitors to long term customers by delivering value and building a loyal base through your affiliates. You will have an affiliate program that will build your business now and in the future.

The goal of Internet marketing is to make it easy for your customer to find you. Given the millions of web sites online, this is becoming a difficult task:

- Search engines give thousands of returns to general searches, which can limit your traffic unless you get to the top of the listings for that specific term.

- Banner ads measure success in terms of CPM (cost per thousand) viewing, a volume approach that can yield lots of traffic, but often mixed results depending on where the banner ad is placed.

Chapter 3

- Posting at newsgroups and mailing lists is a time consuming process that often mixes commercial efforts with non-commercial interests of your customers, which can undermine your efforts.

Early Internet marketing focused on generating high volumes of traffic through concepts like hits (the collective impressions of graphic files and web pages which inflate traffic counts), unique visits (the actual number of visits your web site receives), and clickthroughs from banner ads (the number of times your paid advertisement is clicked on, meaning someone visits your site). Quantity was the focus, not quality.

> **note:** The problem with early marketing systems was that it was difficult to quantify your success.

You could compare sales to number of visitors, but unless your marketing was targeted to a specific audience, the figures would be random at best. Measuring the quality of your traffic, and the success of a particular campaign, was tricky because all marketing was based on taking people from another web site to yours with little in the way of recommendations or referrals, except for links.

In addition, most web sites focused on the model of catalogs and shopping carts, presenting many choices to customers. The fact is, giving people so many choices on first contact leads to more confusion than sales. Shopping carts and catalogs work when the customer is introduced to one product, one service, and given the chance to decide on the offer before checking out the rest of the web site through a home page.

What is needed is a model that drives people to your web site with a specific purpose. Affiliate programs are a natural evolution of Internet advertising towards this goal.

Customers do not surf through the Web for hours as was once assumed. After initial searching, they settle into the few web sites that fulfill their specific interests. These web sites develop a following, build community, and create a feeling of trust and loyalty that is critical to any business' success.

How to generate quality traffic that leads to more sales:

"Online shelf space"

Acting more as a personal recommendation than a random banner ad or link, affiliate programs have the capability of bringing together a motivated audience with a variety of products and services related to their interest. These programs are similar to the idea of shelf space in a retail store:

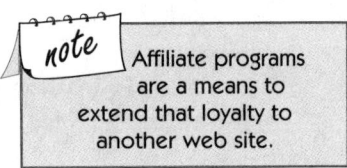

> **note** Affiliate programs are a means to extend that loyalty to another web site.

- The owner of the web site works to get traffic to the online storefront.

- Businesses that want to offer products or services to visitors at this storefront negotiate with the owner of the store to get good placement in areas of the store that customers visit the most.

- Products and services which are related to the specific concept of the storefront—like baseball gloves in sporting good stores—sell better because they are targeted towards a specific interest of that customer base.

- Getting your product in a favorable position at the site—in the right shelf space so it will be noticed and generate interest—is crucial.

Affiliate programs have become an increasingly popular way to gain influence with the customer base you are targeting, by rewarding those who generate the traffic with:

- Per commission sales, paying a referral fee, commission, or simply a percentage of each sale in exchange for someone posting an advertisement at their web site.

Chapter 3

- Per inquiry sales, which pay per visitor or per click through (literally, each time it is clicked) of banner ads. For affiliate programs, per inquiry has been translated to mean the number of times a customer inquires about a specific product or service. CarPrices.com is an excellent example of a company that uses per inquiry advertising.

The key is to find out where your customers are and get them working with you, quickly. You need to set up a foothold in your target customer base. The best way to do this is find the highest traffic sites for your particular product or service, and start developing your Internetwork as quickly as possible.

The concept is quite simple; web sites are the "shelf space" of the Internet. Your goal is to define your customer base, discover where they are meeting, and arrange it so it is easy for them to find you by making it profitable for the owner of that web site—that shelf space—to provide a link to your site. The best way to begin understanding your goals is by answering the following questions:

1) What's your business objective? What can you do for your customers that your competitors can't?

2) What are the specific benefits you deliver to your customers (in two sentences or less)?

3) What are your target goals in terms of sales, savings, and time?

4) What is your customer profile? How would I know one of your prospects if I met him or her?

5) What are the top Internet places to market and joint venture with?

Don't worry if you can't answer these right away, but as you go through this program remember this page and keep on developing your answers to these questions.

73

The key is to focus your interest precisely and develop a sales process that allows the surfing Internet customer to drop in, leave you a message requesting more information, buy your product or service, and give you permission to work with them.

As you build your affiliate program, remember your primary goal:

Build a sales force of affiliates that believe in what you are offering, and back them up with a system that automates the advertising, selling, and delivery of your product line. Make it easy for your affiliates, and their customers, to work with you.

Declan Dunn offers consultations, seminars, and training to Web businesses, developers, ISP's, and consultants. E-mail dunn@activemarket place.com or call (530) 873-3637 with questions. All materials Copyright 1998, 1999 Michael Declan Dunn and ADNet International. All Rights Reserved.

General affiliate program resources

Here are several sites about affiliate programs. I'd say the "king" of affiliate program resources is Allan Gardyne, with his AssociatePrograms.com site. His site is primarily written for people interested in becoming affiliates, but he also has tons of good information for business owners who want to start their own affiliate programs.

http://www.affiliate-announce.com

http://www.associateprograms.com

http://www.affiliatesdirectory.com

http://www.2-tier.com

http://www.refer-it.com

http://www.affiliateforce.com

Chapter 3

http://www.revenews.com

http://www.iccworldwide.com/affiliatewatch/directory/new

Just as a side note, you should browse Allan's affiliate program categories. If you find a product that complements your own product/service, consider signing up as an affiliate for that program and offering that product to your own customers.

Check out these sites, which allow you to build a "web store" related to your product—with all sales from said store generating a commission for you. This could be used to build up a second revenue stream from your existing customers.

http://www.econgo.com

http://www.vstore.com

If you have any interest in operating your own affiliate program, I highly recommend the book from which the above article was excerpted, *What Affiliate Programs Are and How to Put Them To Use For You*. You can read about it at this site:

http://www.activemarketplace.com/w.cgi?insiders-1306!bt

Deploying your own affiliate program

First you need to decide if you want to pay affiliates for advertising (impressions), traffic (click-throughs) or sales—or a combination of any of these. Some services/software won't handle all of these, so make sure you know what you want when you begin evaluating your options.

If you decide to have your own affiliate program, there are two ways you can do it. You can either use an affiliate program service, or you can have software installed on your own server. There are advantages and disadvantages to either of these solutions.

With a service, you don't have the same level of control over the program (in some cases, you don't even get access to your own affiliates) and you have a monthly service charge and/or per-transaction or per-affiliate charge in addition to the initial setup charge

With software, you have much more control and fewer recurring costs, but there is generally more effort required on your part.

Affiliate program services

The best-known programs (from what I've seen):

BeFree: http://www.befree.com

Very sophisticated system, but in my experience not easy to use. Designed more for Fortune 500 companies than for the independent business owner.

Commission Junction: http://www.cj.com

Though I haven't experienced their user's interface, I've heard great things about it from several people. Definitely lower cost than BeFree.

Other programs I've seen around, but I don't have much experience with:

LinkShare: http://www.linkshare.com

ClickBank: http://www.clickbank.com

ClickTrade: http://www.clicktrade.com

PluginGo: http://www.plugingo.com

Everyone's needs are different, but of the above services, I'd say ClickBank is the easiest to implement, but least flexible. BeFree is the most

Chapter 3

powerful, but also the most difficult to use, and most expensive. Commission Junction, PluginGo, and ClickTrade seem to strike a good balance between these two ends of the spectrum—with ClickTrade having the lowest initial cost.

Affiliate program software

I created my own affiliate program software two years ago, and have been involved in the technical aspect of the affiliate program industry ever since. The affiliate program software packages listed below all appear to be good quality software available at reasonable cost.

> **note:** The software must be installed on your web server, so be sure software you purchase supports the operating system (usually Unix/Linux or Windows NT) used on your server.

AssocTrac:	http://www.assoctrac.com
TheAffiliateProgram:	http://www.theaffiliateprogram.com
UltimateAffiliate:	http://www.groundbreak.com
AffiliateZone:	http://www.affiliatezone.com
Pro-Track:	http://www.affiliatesoftware.net
Little Salesmen:	http://www.cgitoolbox.com

Warning: flagrant self-promotion follows!

In addition to the above software, there are two packages I designed myself:

YOAP (Your Own Associate Program):   http://www.palis.com/yoap

77

YOAP is the software I designed two years ago, and I have made a number of improvements to it since then. It's a good, low-cost solution for an affiliate program with 10,000 affiliates or less—but it lacks some of the advanced features (and the advanced price) offered in some of the previously listed packages.

Synergyx: http://www.synergyx.com

Synergyx is designed for businesses selling primarily digital (downloadable) products. As far as I know, it's the only software package available that integrates an affiliate program, a shopping cart (optional), and a password-protected digital product delivery system.

The affiliate program functions offered in Synergyx are much more powerful than those in YOAP; however, if you don't need the integrated shopping cart or digital product delivery system, you'll get more "bells and whistles" with one of the affiliate program packages listed previously.

If you have any questions about either of these packages, just send me an email at paulg@businesstoolchest.com

Communications

4

Communications

New technology helps to provide better customer/prospect communications tools with ever-decreasing costs. While email and email-related technologies certainly would fit in this section, they are important enough to warrant a section of their own (see the "Email" section).

VoiceMail and FAX Services

I wanted to talk about these two separately, but most of the resources for one are also appropriate for the other—so I combined them.

It's very likely your local phone company also offers voice mail services, and there may be some advantages to using the service they offer. I only pay $7.95/month for my voice mail, and that includes a feature that redirects incoming phone calls to my voice mail if I'm on the phone when another call comes in.

If you plan to use a voicemail as the response mechanism for a "two-step" advertising campaign, you'll probably want a longer outgoing message than your local phone company provides.

There are *many* voicemail companies—the below resources are only a small sample of those available. For more options, do a search on the keyword "voice mail" at Yahoo.com or GoTo.com.

I suspect that everyone reading this guide is familiar with the facsimile (fax) machine—they've been around for several years now. The problem many small/home businesses have, though, is keeping the fax line open for faxes 24 hours a day—the fax line is oftentimes shared with either a voice line or a computer modem line.

There are several companies that will receive faxes for you—this allows you to have a "dedicated fax line" without tying up your own phone line. Your customers never get a busy signal when they try to send you a fax, and you don't have to worry about whether you're missing one!

Digitcom Services: http://www.digitcom.net/tollfree.html

Flat rate toll-free voicemail. Less than $20/month for 800/888 + extension or $32-$50/month for 877/888/800 number with no extension.

Ureach: http://ureach.com

Fax, email, phone calls, all of your communications in one place.

LinxCom: http://www.linxcom.com

Unified communications and messaging services that include a web-enabled one-number follow me service, an outsourced small business phone service, and other enhanced services.

Jfax: http://www.jfax.com

Remote fax for $15/month, voicemail for an additional $5/ month. You get a phone number in one of several local areas. When a fax is sent to that number, it's sent to you via email. This is the service I use, and I've been very pleased with it.

DeltaThree: http://www.deltathree.com/products/
                          d3box/index.asp

Store your voice mail, email and faxes all in one place. Retrieve them online or from a regular telephone.

NetMoves: http://www.netmoves.com/cgi-bin/netmovesoffercgi

Allows you to fax documents (PDF, MSWORD, etc.) via email. Also allows you to receive faxes which are then sent to you via email. Costs $6.95/mo or $9.95/month for toll-free fax number.

Boomerang: http://www.boomerang.com

Fax4Free: http://www.fax4free.com

FaxAway: http://www.faxaway.com

Fax-on-demand

Fax-on-demand is a service that allows your customers to request and immediately receive information about your company's products or services— 24-hours a day, with no action on your part. Here's how it works:

The customer calls a number you have given them and enters the number of the desired document. As an example, let's consider someone selling nutritional products, They might have the following documents listed in their literature:

0000   Index / List of all available fax-on-demand documents

1001   Information about our company, and how our supplements are made

2000   Product line summary

2005   Stabilized oxygen

2015	Natural mineral supplement
2020	Enzyme supplements
2025	Multi-vitamin supplement
3000	Testimonials from our customers
4000	Order form

If you were the customer, and wanted information on Vitamins, Minerals, and Enzymes, this is what you would do:

1. You would call the Fax-on-demand number from your fax machine. You would hear a message saying something like this:

"Thank you for calling ABC Nutrition's Fax-on-demand system. In order to use this system, you must be calling from your fax machine. You may select up to three documents during this call. Please select a document number followed by the pound sign."

2. You would then type in (using your fax machine keypad) 2015#

The FOD (fax on demand) system would then reply, "You selected document number two-zero-one-five. If you would like to get another document, please enter the document number followed by the pound sign. If you have selected all the desired documents, just hit the pound sign by itself."

3. You would then type in 2020#

The FOD would reply in the same was as in step #2

4. You would then type in 2025#

Chapter 4

This time the FOD system would say something like, "That was the last document for this call. Please hit the 'Start' or 'Send' button on your fax machine to receive the selected documents."

You would hit the Start/Send button on your fax machine, and the documents would be sent to your fax machine immediately!

There are several companies that offer this service, but shop around for the best price and service. Be sure that you select a service that does not charge on a "per page" basis. You want a flat-rate monthly fee, and you don't want to be charged an exorbitant amount for every update or change you make. Here are a few resources to check out:

Data On Call: http://www.dataoncall.com/

Boomerang: http://www.boomerang.com/

Epigraphx also has online faxing with a "Click, drag and send" interface. Sales and marketing data is automatically captured.

http://www.epigraphx.com/

Fax broadcasting

Fax broadcasting can be very effective. The medium itself invokes a sense of urgency, and response can be very quick—and it's very inexpensive. Be sure you're only sending faxes to your own list or to an "opt-in" list—there are laws against sending unsolicited faxes. Here are a few companies who offer fax broadcasting services:

http://www.2sendit.com/

http://www.dataoncall.com/

http://www.boomerang.com/

http://www.epigraphx.com

http://www.J2global.com

http://www.faxaway.com

http://buynow.jfax.com/jblast

Internet phone

I'm talking about software/services allowing your customer to type your phone number into their computer, hit "Go," and have your phone ring.

When you pick up, they can talk to you through their computer microphone and hear you via their computer speakers—you're on your phone, just like normal. It doesn't cost your customer anything to call you (with some services, there is a per minute charge for certain international calls). The reason this is so nice is that many of your customers only have one phone line—this will allow them to talk to you while looking at your site on the internet.

Of course it works the other way too! You could call them.

Additionally, dialpads make it possible for both people to use their computer microphone and speakers for the call.

Here are three services to check out:

http://www.use-deltathree.com/afax/

http://www.dialpad.com/

http://www.callrewards.com/

Chapter 4

Customer support tools

I read the following statistics on the e-comsupport.com site:

- 67 percent of online customers never complete their purchases due to a lack of real-time customer service, according to a survey of 25 top e-commerce sites. (Source: Net Effect)

- 90 percent of online customers prefer human interaction, and about half of those customers make frequent visits to a site before making a purchase, underscoring the value of live customer service.

- 40 percent of survey respondents said that they would be more comfortable with online purchasing if there was more human contact.

(Source: Jupiter Communications)

The dollar volume of lost sales represented by that first number is staggering! Imagine—two out of three people who begin an order *fail to complete* the order due to lack of real-time customer service. *That* should make people stand up and take notice.

Fortunately, there are a number of tools which allow your internet prospects to communicate with you (or your customer support staff) when they need to. The first of these I will discuss are commonly referred to as "instant message" software. I'll use ICQ as an example.

First of all, you'd go to the ICQ site shown below, and download/install the ICQ software. You'll be assigned an ICQ number. Whenever you're "online," the ICQ network will be aware of your presence.

Now here's where it gets exciting! Say "Jim Brown" is browsing your online catalog, and he runs across a something that interests him, but he's not sure if it will work for him. Then he spies your ICQ number displayed on the web page. Jim uses ICQ too, so he sends you an ICQ "instant message"—1 second later, you get a message alert.

87

You click on the incoming message and send an instant message reply back. Or you initiate a "chat" with Jim, whereby you and he type messages back and forth in real-time. You answer all of Jim's questions to his satisfaction, he thanks you, and then proceeds to your order form to place his order.

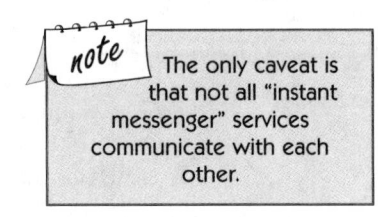

> **note** The only caveat is that not all "instant messenger" services communicate with each other.

Sounds great, doesn't it? In the above scenario, it's quite possible that Jim didn't have ICQ, but used the Microsoft Messenger instead. In that case, you'd need to have MSN Messenger installed on your computer for Jim to contact you.

Fortunately, you can install all of the "big three" instant messenger applications on your computer. You don't need to be an AOL subscriber to use AOL's messenger program. Also good is the price—all three are free!

Here are the sites to visit for your instant messenger software:

ICQ: http://web.icq.com

MSN: http://messenger.msn.com

AIM: http://www.aol.com/aim/

Even though the above programs were really designed for "friends and family" or "interoffice communication" rather than business tools, they lend themselves very well to use in the business world. But it gets even better than that.

Let's consider the above "Jim Brown" scenario again, but imagine this time he doesn't have any instant messenger software on his computer—making ICQ/MSN/AIM totally useless in this case.

Chapter 4

That's okay though, because you have "HumanClick" installed on your system and integrated with your web site (it's very simple to do so). HumanClick allows you to monitor the traffic on your web site and proactively offer your visitor live customer service.

So when Jim comes to your online catalog, you know someone is there. You don't know it's Jim, or anything else about him, but you know someone is looking at your catalog page right at that instant. Now, there are two things that can happen at this point.

1) Jim can click on a "Click Here for Questions" image on your page, which will cause an alert to be sent to you. You can then initiate a real-time chat with Jim. In this respect it's very similar to ICQ et. al.

2) Rather than waiting for someone to click on the "Click Here for Questions" image, you can offer assistance to the visitor. A window will pop-up and inform the visitor that someone is standing by to answer any questions they have.

Keep in mind that Jim doesn't need any "messenger" software installed on his computer to communicate with you via HumanClick. The other software listed below works in a manner similar to what I described above. There may be some differences, but the basic idea is the same for all of them.

HumanClick: http://www.humanclick.com

LiveHelper: http://www.livehelper.com

NetAgent: http://www.eshare.com/products/internet/netagent/index.html

Groopz: http://Groopz.com

All of the above packages are free.

89

The following services cost something:

Jeeves Live: http://corporate.ask.com/products/live.asp

eFusion (Push to talk): http://www.efusion.com/ptt.htm

FaceTime: http://www.facetime.net/products/customer.htm

Like the idea of instant support available to your web visitors, but don't have the resources to "be there" for the live inquiries? One of the following "outsourced" solutions may be just what you need:

E-Commerce Support: http://www.e-comsupport.com

Brigade: http://www.brigade.com

People Support: http://www.peoplesupport.com

eGain.com: http://egain.com

eSupportNow: http://www.esupportnow.com

CustomerDirect: :http://customerdirect.com/bus_services/chat.html

Customer snail-mail

I'm not sure this really deserves to be here—these two resources could be very useful for some people. In case you're really wet behind the ears when it comes to internet jargon, "snail-mail" refers to regular (physically delivered) postal mail.

> **note** Sometimes it's nice to get a real letter from someone rather than one of the various forms of electronic communications.

90

Chapter 4

If you want to send a letter out to your customers, these two resources will surely save you time doing it.

Eletter: http://www.eletter.com

With Eletter, you simply upload your mail list and an electronic version of your document, select from a few options (paper, ink color, etc.) and submit the job. Eletter will print and mail your document to everyone on the list. It's so simple and fast, you'll giggle.

Depending on the quantity and the service you're using, you may even save money by using Eletter—but in most cases you'll be paying a bit more for the convenience.

SuperLetter: http://www.superletter.com

Superletter is similar to Eletter, but doesn't seem to be quite as "polished." You have to download software, then enter the addressee information and letter text into an electronic form, and hit "send." Superletter routes the letter to a terminal in the recipient's country, creates a real (paper) letter, and sends it to the recipient by way of the postal service.

USPS mail online:

http://www.usps.com/mailingonline/

The U.S. Postal Service's "Mailing Online" service appears to work in a manner very similar to ELetter. This service came out just before publication of this guide.

91

Data and equipment protection

5

5

Data and equipment protection

Think about the importance of your computer data. Most businesses have some or all of the following data on their computer:

- customer records
- financial data
- projects under development
- legal documents
- prospective customer contact information
- passwords and account information

Consider all the time, work, and future business represented by this data. The lackadaisical attitude most people have about protecting it simply astounds me!

If you lose this data with no way to restore it, your business will suffer

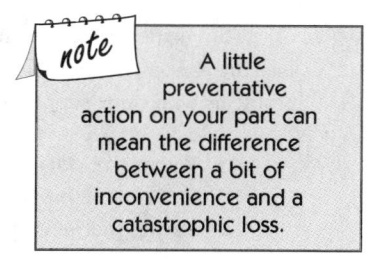

> **note** A little preventative action on your part can mean the difference between a bit of inconvenience and a catastrophic loss.

immensely. You'll spend days or weeks trying to reconstruct what you've lost, and probably will never get back everything. It doesn't have to be—nor *should it* be—that way.

There are three main areas you need to be concerned with:

1) Protection against electrical surges and outages.

2) Protection against disk failure.

3) Protection against viruses and electronic acts of malice.

Protection against electrical surges and outages

Chances are you're already familiar with surge suppressors. You simply plug your computer into a power strip containing surge-suppression circuitry, then plug the power strip into your AC outlet. In the case of a power surge on your AC line, the surge suppression circuitry should redirect the high-current away from your computer. That's the *theory*, anyway.

Before I went into internet work full time, I worked as an electrical engineer designing, implementing, and testing the audio and power distribution circuitry of the Motorola iDen phones. So I can tell you with some authority that when it comes to electricity, there is often a world of difference between "generally accepted theory" and "hard reality."

The "hard reality" is that most surge suppressors are based on a "sacrificial" component called an "MOV" (metal oxide varistor). There are two problems with surge suppressors based on this technology:

1) With each electrical jolt received by an MOV, it loses some of its ability to function properly—eventually it stops functioning altogether, leaving your sensitive computer equipment completely unprotected.

Chapter 5

2) These MOVs are generally employed to divert surge current to "ground*." But current doesn't stop flowing there. This surge current travels through the computer chassis, and up through the "ground reference" lines in your computer's motherboard and other circuitry, through the data ports, etc.

_{* Voltages in a system are usually specified relative to "ground"—just like altitude is generally specified relative to sea level. Ground is simply a "reference" in the electronic system.}

So all the surge suppressor does is prevent the surge from traveling over the "hot" voltage line. The surge still gets to your computer circuitry, just via a different path.

It may interest you to know these surges, even if too small to cause any immediate damage to your system, can affect the data on your computer's data lines—leading to incorrect data, decreased performance, and computer "lock ups" requiring you to reboot your machine.

By the way, don't be fooled by the UL (Underwriters Laboratories) listing on your surge suppressor. It most likely states "UL Listed" or "UL 1449". However, UL standards are primarily safety standards, not performance standards. Your equipment should be UL 1449 listed, because that's a good assurance it won't cause a fire—but it's not an assurance the device will adequately protect your equipment.

So what are you to do? Look for a surge protector with a "UL 1449 *Adjunct* Certified Grade A Class 1 Mode 1" rating. Unlike the standard UL 1449 test, the Adjunct test is an endurance test.

Here are two companies who make surge suppressors complying with the above requirements (they call them "series mode" suppressors):

Brick Wall: http://www.brickwall.com

The company name is actually "Price Wheeler Corporation" but it's their "Brick Wall Division." I have three of these units and have never had a surge problem—even though I live in central Florida, one of the world's lightning "hot spots." I've had several friends here who have had their computer and audio/video equipment damaged from electrical storms—they weren't using very good surge suppressors.

SurgeX: http://www.surgex.com

SurgeX doesn't sell directly to end-users, but you can purchase their surge suppression equipment online at this site:

http://www.systemsstore.com

SurgeX costs more than the BrickWall equipment, but their web site is prettier, so maybe that's okay (Ha!). I don't believe there's any significant difference in the protection supplied by either company as both meet the requirements stated above.

Great, now your equipment is safe against electrical surges in the power lines. But there's still something missing . . . phone line protection.

Chances are, your computer modem is plugged into a phone line. What happens when lightning strikes a nearby phone pole? I think I can sum it up in two words: *burnt toast!* In fact, a lightning strike as far as 1/4 mile away can still induce dangerous voltage levels in wires—if those wires end at your computer, watch out!

There are surge suppressors for phone lines, but unfortunately most of them are based on the same MOV technology discussed earlier. There is one phone line surge suppression device I can recommend, though—the "Optilator."

The Optilator is a device manufactured by Runnels Electronics (in Florida). I assume the name of this device is a combination of the words "optical" and "isolator." Your computer is "isolated" from the phone line by a 4-inch length of fiber-optic cable—definitely non-conductive material!

Chapter 5

Before I knew about the Optilator I would always disconnect from the internet and unplug the phone lines from my computer during a thunderstorm. Now, however, I just keep working. I don't have any concerns about phone-line surges. I have one of these devices on both of my internet-ready computers and have never had any problems.

Here's one online resource where you can purchase an Optilator. I highly recommend you do so.

http://home.earthlink.net/~jpecore/

Power outage counter-measures

It's also a good idea to get an uninterruptible power supply (UPS). Plug your computer into the UPS, plug the UPS into your surge suppressor (if you have one), and plug the surge suppressor into your AC outlet.

The UPS contains a battery, which is kept charged while your home/office power is on. If the power goes out, the UPS converts the battery energy into AC power capable of running your computer. This happens instantaneously, preventing data loss.

Your UPS will provide several minutes of power. If it looks like the outage is going to last longer, you have plenty of time to gracefully exit your currently running applications and shut down the computer.

Most UPS devices include power suppression circuitry, but unless it meets the requirements specified above, you would be wise to get one of the SurgeX or Brick Wall units in addition to the UPS.

Protection against viruses and electronic acts of malice

Computer viruses have been in the news a lot lately, and I expect this will continue for the foreseeable future. The proliferation of script-executing email

99

Online Business Resources Made E-Z

programs has dramatically increased the speed with which one of these viruses is spread throughout the world. If you aren't taking active steps to protect yourself, you're asking for trouble.

Also in the news lately has been a rash of malicious acts by internet "crackers." They've brought several of the most popular internet sites down, and if you don't take measures to stop them, they can tap into your computer as well.

Anti-virus software

Generally speaking, there are two kinds of anti-virus software—scanning and pro-active.

Virus scanning software has been around for awhile. I'm oversimplifying here, but what it does is scan your software programs and compares the program and data code against the "profiles" of known viruses. If it finds a match, it alerts you to the existence of that virus on your system.

> **note**
> Most scanning software comes with a "background" component which scans programs you load in from diskette, CD-ROM, or the Internet.

Here are a few popular anti-virus software packages:

Innoculate It   http://antivirus.cai.com/

Anti-Viral Toolkit Pro: http://www.avp.ch/

Norton AntiVirus: http://www.symantecstore.com

McAfee: http://software.mcafee.com/

"Pro-Active" anti-virus software is relatively new to the scene. The idea is to protect you against viruses which are so new, they haven't even been profiled yet.

> **note:** Pro-active software is especially important if you use email software which automatically launches executable files which have been included in incoming email messages.

The software does this by "isolating" the executing program code and denying it the ability to perform certain functions (such as deleting files, connecting to a network, etc.). If any such attempt is detected, the software alerts you and allows you to grant or deny permission for that action.

For your best protection, you should use both kinds of anti-virus software.

Here are two pro-active anti-virus software packages:

SurfinGate: http://www.finjan.com/

E-safe: http://www.aks.com/esafe/

Anti-cracking software

Most computers today come from the manufacturer with their resource sharing software enabled. This can be a real problem if you happen to be on the internet and someone gains access to your system through one of several software "ports."

How do you find out if you're at risk? Go to this site:

Shields Up: http://grc.com/default.htm

Once you get there, click on the "Shields Up" picture. Then click on "Test my Shields." You'll be given a report on how vulnerable your system is to an intrusion through your internet connection. Also click on "Probe my Ports" for another report about your computer's network ports. If you are vulnerable to an outside attack, you'll be told!

If you discover your computer isn't as secure as you want it to be, here's what to do about it. First, if you're on a Windows PC machine and don't do any file or printer sharing over the internet (that probably covers 99%+ Windows users), there is a very simple solution available to you. Go to this page http://grc.com/su-bondage.htm and follow the instructions to reconfigure your network settings. You can completely isolate your insecure "Microsoft network services" from your internet connection.

If you *do* require file sharing over the internet (including the use of "PCAnywhere" or similar software), then the solution for you is to get your own "firewall" software. Steve Gibson has done lots of research on personal firewalls—you can read all about his findings at this web site: http://grc.com/su-firewalls.htm or, I can just tell you that as of this writing, the best solution for most of us is:

ZoneAlarm: http://www.zonelabs.com/

ZoneAlarm blocks unauthorized entry into your PC, *and* "hides" its ports so nobody knows there's a computer to crack. It also protects you from "spyware," software which runs on your machine and reports your activity to an outside source via the internet. George Orwell would certainly be saying "I told you so" if he were around today.

Protection against disk failure

When it comes to disk failure, there are two things you can do: prevent it and prepare for it. Believe it or not, there *is* software that helps you prevent hard drive failure. If the drive is just too far gone, this software warns you of an imminent failure, giving you time to backup the data on the drive and replace it with a new one. But wait, there's more. If you *do* have a hard drive failure, this software can help you to restore/retrieve your data!

Chapter 5

This software was developed by Steve Gibson, the same guy I talked about in the "anti-cracking software" section. It's called:

SpinRite: http://grc.com/sroverview.htm

One of the testimonials on the SpinRite page suggests data backup is not required if you have SpinRite, but I don't know if I'd ever go that far. I always say better to err on the side of caution. Most of us, sooner or later, will find ourselves in a situation where we will pat ourselves on the back for having a backup of our critical data, or kick ourselves in the butt (repeatedly) for not having it. "Choose wisely."

So with that image emblazoned on the doorway of your memory, consider the following automated backup / online backup resources:

Evault: http://www.evault.com

BlackJack: http://www.backjack.com (Macs only)

Backup.com: http://www.backup.com

Xdrive: http://www.xdrive.com

Connected Online Backup:

http://www.connected.com/solutions/cob_main.htm

($6.95/mo for 100MB storage, $14.95 for unlimited)

Too late, you've already suffered a catastrophic loss? Well, besides SpinRite (discussed above), here's another data recovery package:

EasyRecovery: http://www.ontrack.com/

Discussion groups and diversions

Discussion groups and diversions

Discussion groups

Discussion groups are also known as "Forums" or "Bulletin Boards." These people have made many millions of dollars, so it pays to listen to what they have to say.

Don't be intimidated—go ahead ask questions, and share your observations. This is a very friendly bunch and they know that everyone has something to teach the rest of us. Here are some of the better "small business" and "entrepreneurial" type discussion boards:

> **note** — Discussion groups contain a wealth of information—some of the very best direct marketers visit these sites and unselfishly share their trade secrets.

Entrepreneurial Success Forum (Anthony Blake):

> http://www.ablake.net/forum

Free Publicity: http://www.free-publicity.com/cgi-bin/talk.cgi

GetHigh (traffic): http://gethighforums.com/bin/Ultimate.cgi

Inc.com: http://www.inc.com/discussions

Seeds of Wisdom: http://www.sowpub.com/cgibin/forum/
                   webbbs_config.pl

WilsonWeb: http://www.wilsonweb.com/cgi-bin/ubb/
             Ultimate.cgi

As you might imagine, you can spend quite a bit of time sifting through all the messages on these discussion boards to find messages that will really help you. One site that could save you a lot of time is Leslie Fountain's "BoardWatch." Leslie goes through dozens of discussions, picks out the ones with real "meat" in them, and publishes a daily page of links to those messages.

http://www.friendsinbusiness.com/boardwatch/

Here's a "directory" of over 310,000 discussion groups. Just enter your topic of interest in the search box, and you'll get a list of related discussion groups:

ForumOne: http://www.forumone.com/feature.php

Diversions

I once read the only thing we need to be happy is something to be excited about, something to look forward to, something to be enthusiastic about, etc.

As such, I thought it a good idea to include a few "diversions" from work. You'll be the better for it in all aspects of your life. Admittedly, these reflect my own personal ideas of what is fun, but I'm sure there's *something* here you'd enjoy!

note — We should all take breaks from everyday stress.

Chapter 6

Shopping sites

I don't actually enjoy "shopping" per se, but I do enjoy "buying stuff." Sometimes I've found the anticipation of the UPS delivery is actually more exciting than the actual product once it's here. Like I said, we all need something to look forward to.

http://www.unclaimedbaggage.com

http://www.overstock.com

http://www.edgeco.com

http://www.dak2000.com

http://www.thesharperimage.com

Shopping bots

http://www.mysimon.com

http://www.pricegrabber.com

http://www.consumersearch.com

http://www.dealtime.com

http://www.shopnow.com

http://www.bottomdollar.com

Travel/Vacation

To do your best work, you need to go on vacation once in a while—and dare I suggest a phone-free and email-free vacation? I haven't managed this myself in quite some time, but it sure would be refreshing.

http://www.gorp.com

http://www.nicholsexpeditions.com

http://www.priceline.com

(When the airlines were quoting me ticket prices of $450 to $480, I got them at Priceline for $200!)

http://www.bestfares.com

http://www.cheaptickets.com

Fun and games

Take a 10-minute break once in awhile and try out these "fun sites":

http://www.pogo.com/

http://www.afunzone.com/

http://dir.yahoo.com/Recreation/Hobbies/

http://www.bored.com

http://home.about.com/games/

http://www.2h.com/

http://dir.yahoo.com/entertainment/humor__jokes__and_fun/

Ebook software

7

Ebook software

Ebooks (electronic books) are becoming more popular every day. It's one way you can offer a high-perceived-value giveaway on your site with very little cost to you. Lots of people are doing this as a way to build their opt-in email lists.

There are a number of software programs which allow you to create an ebook. I have listed a few of the better known packages below:

Adobe Acrobat® is my preferred software for creating ebooks. The software creates compact PDF files which can be viewed on virtually any computer and operating system. It also allows you to password protect your document, as well as disable copy/paste and print functions.

People will still be able to copy your file and send it to a friend, though. I personally don't worry too much about this. I think the money I'd lose by offering a less universal file format is more than what I'll lose from people passing my information on to a friend.

http://www.adobe.com/products/acrobat/main.html

HyperMaker Pro / WebPacker: Both of these are made by Bersoft, and if software piracy counter-measures are important to you, one of these would be my recommendation. Sorry, these files can't be used on a Mac. They are only for PC/Windows computers..

WebPacker requires Internet Explorer 4 (or higher) to be loaded on the customer's computer, enabling it to work with all the content/media types available through that browser. HyperMaker doesn't require IE4, nor does it support advanced media content such as Flash, Javascript, etc.

http://www.bersoft.com/hmhtml/

E-ditor Pro compiles HTML files into ebooks. Like most ebook creation software, the resulting files are only usable on a PC/Windows computer. It also requires Internet Explorer 4 or higher. E-ditor Pro does have some nice security features, including the ability to lock specific pages of the document. I've heard some good things about this software.

http://www.e-ditorial.com/software.html

"E-Book HTML Compiler Pro" has two versions. One requires Internet Explorer 4 (or higher) and the other doesn't. The IE4-dependent version can render any content IE4 recognizes (including Javascript, Flash, etc.). This software also has some anti-piracy provisions. Creates PC/Windows ebooks only.

http://www.steveseymour.co.uk/ebook/index.html

Though NeoBook doesn't support some of the media types supported in the various IE4-dependent packages, it does have a very professional look and feel. With some third-party software it can have some very robust security features. Definitely worth your consideration.

http://www.neosoftware.com/nbw.html

Corey Rudl's "ebookpro" is a relatively recent addition to this category. The main advantage of this package is its anti-privacy measures, and in this regard it's an impressive piece of software. From what I can tell, ebooks created with this software will only work on a Windows PC with Internet Explorer 4 or higher.

Chapter 7

> One drawback (in my opinion) is the requirement to purchase registration numbers for each ebook you distribute. I understand the company's need to require this (as they are providing ongoing anti-privacy protection for you) but I guess as a matter of personal preference, it just "rubs me the wrong way."

http://www.ebookpro.com

Winebook is a very basic (and inexpensive) ebook compiler. It converts RTF files into PC/Windows compatible ebooks.

http://superwin.com/super.htm

WebCompiler is the new version of InfoCourier, one of the first ebook compiler packages available. It has some security/anti-piracy features, but I don't think they're as good as HyperMaker/WebCompiler or EbookPro. Like the others (except for Adobe Acrobat), it creates ebooks which are only readable on a Win/PC platform. It requires the user to have Windows 98/2000 or Windows 95/NT4 + Internet Explorer 4 or higher.

http://www.smartcode.com/icour.htm

WebExe is another "basic" HTML compiler. Not much in the way of security, and no Mac support. I can't tell for sure from the website, but I believe it only handles HTML text, images, and sound. I didn't see anything about other media types or JavaScript.

Efficiency/ productivity boosters

8

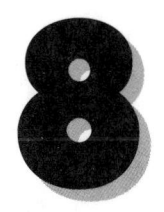

Efficiency/ productivity boosters

Nobody has enough time these days, so anything we can do to *save* time is worth looking at. I expect you won't be able to use all of the resources below, but there will be *some* you will find very useful.

I expect this section in the members-only section to grow by leaps and bounds once I get a few people contributing links to their favorite time-savers. So be sure to check back often!

Optimized windows performance

If you use a PC, there aren't many things more frustrating than a system crash. A number of utilities claim to help prevent crashes, but some of them seem to do more harm than good.

One utility I've been using with success is "ReleaseRam." ReleaseRam is advertised as a program to make your system run faster through memory recovery. A "side benefit" is that you may have fewer system crashes.

ReleaseRam: http://www.releaseram.com

Online "surfing" assistants

Online "surfing assistants" run on your computer while you're online and give you useful information related to whatever site you happen to be on. This can save you time searching for information in other ways.

Online Business Resources Made E-Z

FlySwat: When you are surfing with FlySwat running, you can click on any word on the currently displayed web page, and FlySwat will give you a list of clickable links related to that word.

http://www.flyswat.com

Gurunet: GuruNet is a lot like FlySwat, but there's one major difference —you can use it with any text document, not just web pages. For instance, if you are reading a report in your word processor, you can click on a word in that report and GuruNet will go out and find web links related to that word. You have to be connected to the internet, of course!

http://atomica.com

Alexa: While the above two programs are word-centric, this program is webpage-centric. In their own words, "It works with your browser to provide essential information about each product you consider and each site you visit." The information they're talking about is related sites, freshness, speed, traffic, contact information, and more. Great tool for researching your possible JV partners and/or competitors!

http://www.alexa.com

BullsEye2: This program is more like a searching assistant with a built-in browser to view your results. You enter a search term and it looks through its database of over 800 search engines for matching entries. Before displaying the results, it removes all "dead links" and pages with no relevant content. After you get the results, you can refine your search within those same results. Once you've found what everything you needed, you can store the results in a hyperlinked report. Really a very nice research tool.

http://info.intelliseek.com/prod/be_download.htm

Gator and Obongo: These two utilities keep an internal record of your personal information, username/password information for various online sites

120

you belong to, and more. When you get to an online form (like an order form or a username/password screen), they fill it in for you.

http://www.gator.com

http://www.obongo.com

iMarkup: Have you ever gone back to a bookmarked web site and asked yourself, "Why did I bookmark this site?" iMarkup helps solve that problem by allowing you to attach "sticky notes" to a web page. When you go back to the web page, the sticky notes pop up right at the location you stuck them. Cool.

http://www.imarkup.com

Optimized browser performance

There are a number of software programs for optimizing your internal Windows communications configurations for the best possible modem performance.

SpeedLane: http://www.speedlane.com

This one isn't software, it's a little "electronic noise filtering" device you hook up between your phone line and your modem. The company guarantees a connectivity performance increase or your money back!

ModemShark: http://modemshark.safeshopper.com/

Miscellaneous productivity tools

If you find yourself typing the same phrases over and over (such as your address information, company name, etc.) you can speed things up with a keystroke macro utility called "shortkeys."

http://www.shortkeys.com

Have you ever had a big file downloading and then lose your connection at the 95% completed mark? (I can almost hear you people with cable modems and DSL lines chortling.) Well, here are a couple of programs to ease your pain. These programs act as "download managers." You can schedule downloads for later, resume interrupted downloads, and more.

http://www.gozilla.com

http://www.getright.com/

If you do a lot of web surfing, your browser's list of favorite sites (a.k.a. bookmarks) has probably grown so large it's not very useful anymore. What to do? Grab a copy of "PowerMarks." PowerMarks imports your list(s) and creates an index of keywords. When you know you visited a site about "garden tools," but you don't remember the URL, just open your PowerMarks window and start typing.

Once you type in "g" it will show all the sites with keywords starting with "g." Then type "a"—it drops all the sites that don't have keywords beginning with "ga." At this point, you may be able to spot the site you're looking for—if not, keep typing. By the time you've typed "garden tools" there should only be a few sites showing.

Not only does it do this, but it also does regular checks on the web sites to see if they've changed at all. Take it from me, it's a very useful tool to have.

http://www.kaylon.com/power.html

Spam countermeasures

If you find unsolicited commercial email taking *too* much of your time, here are some tools to help you get it under control:

MailExpire: This description comes right from their website: "Our system allows you to create a free email alias for yourself. For a period you choose, from 12 hours to a month, anything sent to this email alias will be passed on to you at your actual email address. You can now give this alias to that salesman you're not sure of. If you get appropriate email from him, that's great. However, if you start receiving spam, you know where it came from, and you only have to put up with it until your alias expires."

> **note** Unsolicited commercial email is requiring an ever-increasing amount of time to dispose of, and that's not because the disposal process takes any longer—it's because the volume of UCE is going up.

http://www.mailexpire.com

Spam Buster: This one operates with your existing email account. In their own words: "Customize filters for selecting exactly which emails you want deleted. Also applies a list of over 15,000 known spammers and optionally uses DNS lookup to validate addresses."

http://www.contactplus.com/products/spam/spam.htm

Email related tools and resources

9

Email related tools and resources

In my opinion, email is still the internet's only "killer app"—but if you can't maintain control over it, that term can take on a whole new meaning. The tools/resources discussed in this section help you to automate your email communication, freeing up more time for promotion, customer service, and product development.

Personal email software

Your first email-related consideration should be what software program you're using for your basic email tasks.

If you don't have/use this feature, you risk losing an important message in the email avalanche descending on your "inbox" each day as well as email-induced fatigue, irritability, and a general sense of "overwhelmedness."

> **note** Don't even think about using an email program unless it has *filtering* capabilities—this is the key to managing incoming emails with efficiency.

There are many email programs, but three of the most popular are:

Eudora: http://www.eudora.com

Pegasus: http://www.pmail.com/

Outlook: http://www.microsoft.com/office/outlook/

All of these have email filtering capabilities. The first two are free. Eudora is advertiser-supported, and Pegasus is just plain free (I use Pegasus myself). Outlook is included in the Microsoft Office product. A "lite" version (Outlook Express) is included in the Windows operating systems as well.

List servers

The beauty of the list server is all the time and work it saves you:

- You send one single, solitary email to your list server email address and it's copied and sent out to hundreds, thousands, or even millions of people.

- Generally someone "signs up" to be on your distribution by sending a blank email to your list server's subscription email address, or by submitting a form from a web site

- Any "bounced" (invalid) email addresses are removed from the list automatically.

- Retries to temporarily unavailable email addresses are executed automatically.

- All subscribe and unsubscribe requests are handled automatically.

note Once the list server is setup, all you worry about is how to get more people to signup for the list and what email to send your list next. It's *sweet*.

Typical uses for a list server are newsletters, electronic magazines (e-zines), news lists, customer lists, and opt-in list advertising.

There are a number of free list server services, but their own advertising appears on each recipient's email. Generally it's not too intrusive, and as long as your list is 5000 people or less, these might be a good way to start out. Three of the best known are:

Topica: http://www.topica.com

ListBot: http://www.listbot.com

Egroups: http://www.egroups.com

If you have a large list, or just want more control and more powerful features (such as merging the recipient's name into the message for a "personal" touch), here are some reasonably priced options. Be sure to read about their features. The "merging" feature I mentioned above is available at sparklist.com, but you'll have to check the others.

SparkList: http://www.sparklist.com

SlingShot: http://www.slingshotmedia.com

Dundee: http://www.dundee.net/isp/commercial.html

PostMaster General: http://www.postmastergeneral.com/

Email merging / distribution software

If you don't want to pay any recurring charges to distribute your e-zine, you're in luck. You can do it all from your own computer. It takes longer and isn't quite as automated as when you use a service, but you only pay once.

In addition to sending your email to a list of subscribers, these three programs allow you to merge recipient information into your outgoing message.

WorldMerge: http://www.coloradosoft.com/

Aureate Group Mail: http://www.infacta.com/gm.html

MailKing: http://www.messagemedia.com/solutions/mailking/

Autoresponders services

Sometimes referred to as an "email robot," an autoresponder is the email equivalent of a Fax-on-demand system. Someone sends an email to your autoresponder email address, and your autoresponder immediately sends them a predefined message via email.

If you don't have enough—or the right kind of autoresponder as part of your standard hosting service, one of these companies should be able to help you out:

> *note* — When looking for an autoresponder, first check with your web hosting provider. Many accounts come with 1, 2, 10 or even unlimited autoresponders.

InfoBack: http://www.infoback.net

DataBack: http://www.databack.com/mailback.htm

Sequential email services and software

Your highest sales potential will only be realized through consistent and repeated follow-up of your prospects—and that's what sequential email services and software is all about.

Here's how it works:

1. Your prospect sends an email inquiry or submits a simple inquiry form on your web site.

2. The prospect receives an immediate reply from your system.

3. The prospect's name/email is added to a queue for follow-up messages.

4. After 2 days (or whatever time period you specify), the prospect receives a followup email. Then 3 days later, another. Then another ... and so on until your cycle of sales messages has been completed.

Note that the prospect has the option of "opting out" of the sequence at any time, and if chosen to do so, the prospect is immediately and automatically removed from the queue.

The higher the price of your product/service, this more important this kind of system is—but everyone should use it. The difference it can make in your closing ratio can be phenomenal.

Like most internet-related tools, you can opt for a service (more automation and a monthly cost) or your own software (less automation—no monthly cost).

Sequential email services:

Aweber: http://www.aweber.com
(one of the first, and still the most popular)

GetResponse: http://www.getresponse.com
(less expensive than Aweber)

PostMasterOnline: http://www.postmasteronline.com/home/11038 (affiliate link)
(relatively new, but very powerful features)

Sequential email software:

Pipeline: http://www.pipelinemail.com

PostMaster: http://post-master.net/rs/Index/index.shtml

MailLoop: http://www.mailloop.com

SPA: http://www.scamfreezone.com/t.cgi/
118203/impact/ (affiliate link)

T.E.A.S.*: http://www.groundbreak.com/s/tr_index.html
* "Timed Email Autoresponder System"

Ezines (electronic magazines)

10

10
Ezines (electronic magazines)

Distributing your own electronic magazine or newsletter is an excellent way of cultivating your customer relationships—but it does require some commitment on your part. Don't promote it as a "weekly" ezine unless you actually have the time and discipline to write one and send it out every week—I'm talking from sad experience here.

I'd like to start out with an excellent article from someone who currently publishes no fewer than six ezines (I'd say she's qualified), Shery Ma Belle Arrieta. Shery's article includes most of the resources I had planned for this section, plus several I didn't know about. I do have just a few more after the article.

HOW TO START YOUR OWN EZINE IN EIGHT STEPS

by Shery Ma Belle Arrieta

Copyright © 2000

Are you a writer? A business owner? A webmaster? Or maybe someone with information you want to share? What better way to promote anything you have than through a newsletter?

No matter how many promotional strategies are developed for the Internet, email is still going to rule. Why do you think email newsletters are sprouting like mushrooms? They wouldn't be leaping by the numbers everyday if there aren't any markets or audience for ezines.

> **note** If "Information is King" on the Internet, then email is king of all promotional media on the Internet.

So how do you go about starting your own ezine or newsletter? Here are the basic eight steps:

1) Know what kind of ezine you want to produce and why. Ask yourself these questions:

- Why would I want to start my own ezine?

- What kind of information or content will I put there?

- What kind of resource, knowledge or information do I have that's uniquely mine and that which other people need?

- How do I create a need for the kind of information I have?

2) Know your audience. Once you have determined what kind of ezine you want to produce, ask yourself these questions:

- Will my ezine have a target age range?

- If my ezine is for writers, what kind of writers will they be? Freelance? Beginners? Technical writers? Working writers?

- If I'm going to promote my products and services in the ezine, what other outside information can I add to keep my readers interested?

- Is my ezine going to be region-specific or global?

Chapter 10

Subscribe to ezines similar to the one you are planning to start. Note which articles are published, how the ezine is presented, how advertisements are written, and how all these are presented with the ezine's audience in mind.

3) Once you've identified your readers, learn where to find them. Before you even start your ezine, have an ezine promotion plan ready. Know where you'll be promoting your ezine.

If you're starting an ezine, go ahead and sign up for these announcement lists:

Get More Subs: getmoresubs-subscribe@egroups.com

Sites and Zines: sitesandzines-subscribe@egroups.com

Smart Announce: smart-announce-subscribe@egroups.com

Announce List: announce-subscribe@egroups.com

Ezines Today: ezinestoday-subscribe@egroups.com

Zine Directory: ZineDirectory-subscribe@egroups.com

For an even more comprehensive list of where you can announce, promote and find subscribers, send an email to FreeAdsReport @fastfacts.net, the *List Announcement Report* by Angela Giles Klocke. This report is updated, with new announcement lists added on a regular basis.

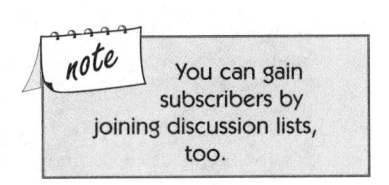

> **note:** You can gain subscribers by joining discussion lists, too.

Participate in discussions. Take advantage of your signature file. Put your ezine's info and subscription email on it. The more active you are, the more people will see your sig file. Even if you've not set the

137

date of your ezine's first issue, it's never too early to promote your ezine and make people aware of it.

Since you're observing all those other ezines you've subscribed to, you might as well contact the owners and find out if they put out free ads. Also, it won't hurt if you submit free articles for publication. Most ezines are non-paying but they pay writers another way: free advertising in exchange for an article. This will help you attract more subscribers.

4) Decide how frequently you'll publish and send out your ezine. If you decide to publish it on a monthly basis, then be sure to send it on time. Be prompt. If you decide to send out your ezine every month, stick to this.

Avoid sending out separate announcements. Your subscribers will be subscribing to your ezine with the knowledge that they'll get it once a month, so think twice before you send out short emails, no matter how urgent they are.

However, there'll be times when you won't be able to meet your deadline. Don't leave your subscribers hanging. Inform them that you will be unable to come out with an issue.

5) Decide upon your ezine's content. You can write original articles for your ezine, and you can also consider using free articles.

A number of places on the Internet offer free articles. Using articles freely provided by their authors is a good way to create an image that you have contributors. Some writers are willing to have their articles published for free in exchange for having their resource boxes published along with their article. It's a win-win situation between you and your guest writers.

Here's a list of where you can look for free articles:

Ezine Articles: http://www.ezinearticles.com

Chapter 10

Publish In Yours: publishinyours-subscribe@onelist.com

Media Peak http://www.mediapeak.com

Free Content: free-content-subscribe@onelist.com

IdeaMarketers: http://www.ideamarketers.com

Worldwide Information Outlet:
http://www.certificate.net/wwio

Internet News Bureau: http://www.newsbureau.com

Internet Wire: http://www.internetwire.com

6) Decide if you will completely be email-based or you will have a complementing web site. If you decide to have a web site, be sure to update it and work on it on the same frequency as you will work on your email newsletter. You will need to know some HTML in order to do this.

> *note* — Never depend on free content to run your ezine. Make sure you publish one or two original articles you've written.

There are several web sites that offer free tutorial on web page building.

7) Using a list manager can help you with your subscriber list. There is list management software available for a fee. However, if you are on a shoe-string budget, you can use the free web-based list management services of eGroups/ONElist http://www.egroups.com, Topica http://www.topica.com, and Listbot http://www.listbot.com.

If you're new to the concept of how mailing lists work, the article *Email Lists: Lurk, Speak Up, Jump Right In!* explains how lists

139

work, the types of lists, and how you can sign up and start your own list. It's available by autoresponder. Send an email to elists@sendfree.com.

8) Ok, so you now have your first issue ready to go out in public. You've followed the first seven steps and managed to get subscribers. The next thing to do is to list your ezine in ezine directories. This will help you gain even more exposure.

Here are ezine directories you can list your ezine in:

E-zineZ.com:	http://www.e-zinez.com
Directory Of Ezines:	http://www.lifestylespub.com
Liszt:	http://www.liszt.com/submit.html
Ezine Seek:	http://www.ezine-unbiverse.com
eZINE Search:	http://www.ezinesearch.com
Inkpot's Zine Scene:	http://www.inkpot.com
E-Zines Today:	http://www.ezine-news.com
Zine World:	http://www.oblivion.net/zineworld

Getting that first issue out isn't the end of your being an ezine publisher. If you want exposure, more subscriptions, and success for you and your ezine, you will need to continue writing, promoting, writing, promoting, writing, promoting . . . .

Shery Ma Belle Arrieta is a writer, editor, web designer, publisher and ebook author currently based in the Philippines. She has been publishing ezines since October 1998. To date, she publishes six ezines—three of which are ezines geared for writers, the fourth is an inspirational ezine, the fifth is an ezine for webmasters, netpreneurs and ezine publishers, and the sixth is an ezine about Internet in the Philippines. She is the managing editor of EbookSpecials.com, a newly-launched ebookseller in the Philippines. Visit her websites at: http://www.sheryarrieta.com, http://suite101.com/welcome.cfm/beginning_writers, and http://msc.edu.ph/wired. Email her at writer@ewritersplace.com.

Great resource, rich article. Here are a few more related resources:

There's a nifty "Ezine Builder" at this URL:

http://www.e-zinez.com/freezine/index.html

Here are some newsletter filler / content services to help you when you just can't seem to fill in all the blank space on your computer monitor:

http://www.ezinearticles.com

http://www.ezinenewswire.com

http://www.inc.com/users/QuickCopy-ds.html

Ezines to subscribe to and read

These are some of the best business related ezines I've run across. You can study these ezines to get some ideas about layout, formatting, content, etc. for your own ezine.

> **note** You can get a very good education by reading these ezines and and applying the knowledge found therein.

I suggest you subscribe to several (dare I say all?) of these. Read them all for a few issues and then unsubscribe from any which don't hold your interest. By the way, this isn't even the tip of the iceberg—there are thousands of business-related ezines—and that's probably a relatively small category.

Note: To find more ezines in this or any other category, be sure to check out the list of ezine directories in the "advertising" section of this guide.

All the Secrets: http://www.ozemedia.com

AskNetrageous.com: http://www.asknetrageous.com/

Associate Programs Newsletter:
>http://www.AssociatePrograms.com/
search/testimonials.shtml

BizWeb Gazette: http://www.bizweb2000.com/sample.htm

ClickZ: http://www.clickz.com/

Doctor Ebiz: http://www.doctorebiz.com/

ProfitInfo: http://profitinfo.com/freesub.htm

Sell It! E-Commerce Weekly: http://sellitontheweb.com/

Web Digest For Marketers: http://wdfm.com/

Web Marketing Today: http://www.wilsonweb.com/wmt/

I-Sales Digest: http://www.adventive.com

Fulfillment, help sites, & Internet marketing

Fulfillment, help sites, & Internet marketing

You love getting orders, but feel you're spending an inordinate amount of time filling them. If you don't implement some kind of automation in this aspect of your business, your growth will undoubtedly be limited.

> **note** Order fulfillment can sometimes be a business owner's biggest headache.

The companies below will take over as many of your order fulfillment responsibilities as you care to give them. They'll take the calls (or get the order notification emails), authorize the credit card transaction, create an invoice, pack and ship the product to the customer, and send you a daily order summary.

If you only want to make use of their order-taking services, most can accommodate you. Or if you prefer they *only* do the packing/shipping, that can be arranged too. The only company I've personally worked with is Ifulfill.com. I've been very happy so far with their service and reliability. While I don't have any personal experience with the other companies, they have received high marks by others.

Ifulfill.com: http://www.ifulfill.com

Shipping-and-Handling: http://shipping-and-handling.com

Customer Direct: http://customerdirect.com

StarByte: http://www.starbyte.com

Moulton Logistics: http://www.moultonlogistics.com/jsindex.asp

Allfulfillment: http://www.allfulfillment.com

Express Fulfillment: http://www.expressfulfillment.com/Fulfillment.htm

Technipak: http://www.technipak.com

UDSI: http://www.udsi.com

Customer Direct: http://customerdirect.com

Hartford Fulfillment: http://www.hartforddirect.com

PMDS: http://www.pmds.com

Aero Fulfillment: http://www.aerofulfillment.com

TFG Direct: http://www.tfgdirect.com

Total Response: http://www.totalresponse.com

Karol Media: http://www.karolmedia.com

Progressive Dist.: http://www.prodist.com/

ClickShipDirect: http://www.clickshipdirect.com

Mimeo*: http://www.mimeo.com

Chapter 11

Mimeo is a special case you can use when you need to get a printed product out right away and have none in stock. You simply upload the document file to their server and they'll print, bind, and ship it to your customer via FedEx. If you get your document to them by 10 PM Eastern, it will be to your customer the next day! It costs more (as single quantity rush orders generally do) but its convenience can't be beat.

Help sites

A number of sites offer help in various areas. Some are free, while some cost money—usually a very reasonable amount (and you never pay anything until/unless you've agreed to a paid service).

HelpTalk is a group of discussion groups related to application software. For instance, there are groups for Microsoft Word, Quicken, Access, Windows 95/98, Corel Draw, and lots more. This is an excellent resource.

http://www.helptalk.com/index.html

You may have heard of the *Service Corps Of Retired Executives* [SCORE] before. They too have a web site. If you have questions about running your business, these people have ample experience to draw upon.

http://www.score.org/

Ask.com (formerly AskJeeves) is somewhat like a "meta search engine," but different. Great place to start when you have a question about how to do something. (Free)

http://ask.com

ZDNet is a good place to go with questions of a technical nature. (Free)

http://www.zdnet.com/zdhelp

147

TechKnowHow offers free reference material and optional for-pay help. They have $9.95 and $19.95/month service plans as well as a per-incident phone help plan.

http://www.techknow-how.com/

AllExperts is free, and guarantees an answer to your question from one of their volunteer experts within 3 days. Most answers are within 1 day.

http://www.allexperts.com/

The following resources act as an "exchange" for you and an "expert" who can help you with whatever problem you may be having. The rates are set by the expert.

http://www.exp.com

http://www.expertcity.com

http://www.experts.com

Internet marketing

There's no shortage of information about internet marketing. It amazes me how quickly some people jump from "new in internet marketing" to calling themselves "internet marketing experts." I've been involved in internet marketing for a few years now and I know "a heckuvalot," but I *still* don't consider myself worthy of the label "expert." However, I *do* consider myself fairly well-read on the subject and am happy to recommend some of the best information I've run across on the topic.

Most internet marketing books and courses are promoted via affiliate programs. These are no exception, and I've taken the liberty of including my own affiliate number in some of these links. If you really chafe at the idea of me getting any more of your hard earned money, just remove everything after ".com" or ".net."

Chapter 11

EnlowCircle Membership. Mike Enlow is one of the pioneers of electronic marketing. More information is here than anywhere else—not just printed information, but downloadable audio and video clips. This requires a higher investment than the other products listed on this page, but it's also the least expensive on a dollar-per-byte basis. It's just excellent information, all around.

http://www.enlowcircle.com/go/1050

Jonathan Mizel's Newsletter. You get over 500 pages of "back issues" and other information, plus a monthly newsletter with the latest techniques from this highly-respected internet marketer.

http://www.activemarketplace.com/w.cgi?mizel-1306

Corey Rudl's big course. This course contains the methods and techniques Corey has used to become one of the best known internet marketers.

http://www.marketingtips.com/tipsltr.html

Right On the Money. In this, book Patrick Anderson shows you a common-sense approach for quickly generating online revenues.

http://www.activemarketplace.com/w.cgi?righton-1306

The Amazing Formula That Sells Products Like Crazy by Marlon Sanders. Measured in "bang for the buck," this Internet marketing book is one of the best available.

http://www.higherresponse.com/track/t.cgi/8338

Ken Evoy has published several books now, all about Internet marketing. These include "Make Your Site Sell," "Make Your Price Sell," and "Make Your Words Sell." It has been a bit unnerving to some of my information-marketing peers that Ken sells these books for so little money--but there's no denying the high quality and value of the information.

http://www.sitesell.com/pg.html

Joint ventures

12

12

Joint ventures

I wanted to include a section on this very powerful method of marketing, and the best resource I could come up with is the below article from Mike Enlow. While the focus of Mike's article is on how to arrange joint ventures between other businesses, Mike gives enough examples of different JV arrangements that it's useful to business owners who are considering their own joint venture. I don't know anyone with more experience and knowledge about joint venture arrangements, and I'm very grateful to Mike for allowing me to reproduce his article here.

"Sandcastles to Empires"

By Mike Enlow

How to start with nothing and create great wealth

Preface

Few believe me when I tell them of the fortunes they can make starting with nothing.

My system is simple. It makes use of the fact that most people don't understand or appreciate what it takes to create more wealth and income: Use their own existing business assets or other's overlooked assets!

"I am appalled at how few business owners leverage off of their hard earned assets. Fortunes have been made by following my simple step-by-step system. This creates wealth for everyone. My program is not a self serving 'I win and you lose' program. It is a program where I share my incredibly simple techniques for creating profit centers, starting from scratch, where everyone wins." *Michael E. Enlow*

"The teacher, if indeed wise, does not bid you enter the house of their wisdom, but leads you to the threshold of your own mind." *Kahil Gibran*

How to create wealth from other's overlooked assets and be the "knight in shining armor" for doing it!

Sometimes I feel like I have the only pair of "macroscopic glasses" (to see the big picture) when examining businesses and the many opportunities for creating additional cash flow.

Almost every business I consult has no less than 3 (and often 10) different ways to almost immediately create additional cash flow from their existing efforts, clients and advertisements.

What I will be sharing with you is one of the simplest of these concepts. I call it "Joint Venture Alliances" or Co-Ventures. I will assume you have no knowledge of marketing (for the benefit of those of you who are less familiar with my marketing techniques).

Let's begin.

Chapter 12

I've discovered many working marketing concepts and systems. All of them are centered around one thing—leverage! They are centered around how to use leverage to get greater profits and greater satisfaction out of every dollar spent and every effort expended.

Over the years, I've learned every business has one need in common—the need to create more cash flow than they spend on overhead. Tens of thousands of businesses do this very successfully. Unfortunately, they overlook many opportunities to gain greater leverage and reap greater rewards from what they do. It takes just as much energy to create an advertisement that gets 100 sales (or leads) as it does to get 1000. I teach how to test headlines, packaging, pricing, etc. to gain greater leverage on your advertising. However, this report is going to address one of the fastest and easiest ways you can teach almost any business owner to *increase his or her profits by as much as 300%,* and do so with nobility.

One of the most ridiculous mistakes and oversights in marketing is the failure to recognize the true value of the relationship a business owner has with his or her customers, vendors and others dealt with on a daily basis. Properly utilizing this overlooked asset can mean thousands, and often tens of thousands of dollars, in increased revenue.

I'll explain.

When someone makes a purchase, they prefer buying from someone they trust and who has treated them fairly in the past. If I were to rent a "cold list" (a list of names of people who know nothing about me, my company, product, service or offer) I may, with a well crafted sales letter or presentation, get a 1 to 3 percent response to the offer. However, if you go to the owner of that same list and structure a deal where the owner writes or presents the *very same offer,* you will see a response that is so much greater it boggles the mind. I've seen responses to this type of offer (we'll call this an "endorsed offer") that skyrocket to as high as 33%!

Accordingly, you can literally earn a fortune by showing others how to use this principle by creating win/win deals. A good example of using this concept happened this past Christmas with a client of mine who is in the pharmacy business. My client had approximately 10,000 customers on file, all of whom loved and trusted my client for the excellent service they had received over the years. However, I discovered my client never ever used this asset of trust to do a noble win/win deal.

> **note** — By doing a Joint Venture, wherein they recommend or refer their customers to another professional and noble company, they could take a percentage of the profits from the newfound business they create for the company they endorse.

Unfortunately too many business people are myopic (nearsighted—cannot see the big picture) when they're observing their business. They fail to realize that although they sell pharmaceutical products and supplies, all their customers still purchase other products and services like dry cleaning, groceries, cars, insurance, accounting services, etc. The relationship with their customers provides a business owner with the incredible opportunity to use the "endorsed offer."

In this particular situation I learned they were friends with a jeweler in town and Christmas was rapidly approaching. I saw an instant jackpot. By the way, these deals can be created without a prior relationship with the vendor you will endorse.

Here's a brief overview of what can happen with Joint Ventures or "Endorsed Offers."

I immediately contacted the jeweler to get the "golden nuggets" to create a letter for my pharmacy clients to share with their customers. I learned he regularly flew to New York to purchase diamonds, emeralds, rubies and other precious stones but, more importantly, he purchased in quantity by teaming up with a fellow jeweler in New Orleans. He literally saved a fortune by buying in bulk.

Chapter 12

We drafted a letter something like this:

Dear Customers and Friends,

Last week my wife and I were browsing through the many Christmas card binders to select a suitable Christmas card to mail to you, our customer, to express our appreciation for your patronage.

Of the many hundreds of Christmas cards we had to select from, we couldn't find a single card that expressed our heartfelt feelings and appreciation for you as a customer. After all, it is customers like you that helped us to send our two children through college and build our business to be one of the most successful pharmacies in the city. Frankly, I decided to say thank you in a very special way—with actions, not words.

Let me explain.

One of my dearest friends is a local jeweler, who has the largest selection of diamonds, rubies, emeralds, watches, and other inventory in the area, but more importantly, he has developed an incredible method of wholesale purchasing that allows him to save a fortune.

As we were talking, I explained how I wanted to do something very special for my friends and customers this Christmas that would express my gratitude for your business. I further explained how I wanted to do something that would benefit you and thus express my thanks with actions rather than just words in a Christmas card.

After a bit of "arm twisting" he agreed to allow my customers who bring in this letter to his store, during their Christmas shopping, to receive a 20% discount! This is good for any purchase you may wish to make this year. In doing this I am saying "thank you" in my own special way. Since he is providing you with the finest quality jewelry, he believes that you will continue to be his customer for years to come. He agreed.

> So, feel free to take this letter to XYZ Jewelers anytime between now and Christmas, and you will receive a "privileged discount" of 20 percent off any purchases as well as VIP treatment from my friend. Since almost everyone buys jewelry during Christmas, my wife and I felt this to be a much better way of saying thank you than any card we may ever send.
>
> Enjoy, and Merry Christmas.
>
> Don and Susan Smith, XYZ Pharmacy
>
> PS. Oh yeah, he did request that I ask you to "slide this letter" to him in an inconspicuous way so his other customers won't feel slighted. They aren't getting this VIP discount. Please do me this kind favor when you go in.

This letter of endorsement became the pharmacy's "Christmas Card" for this past year. We had pre-arranged a special deal where XYZ Pharmacy would receive half of the new found profits from everyone who came in. Because of that we earned an incredible $87,550 mailing Christmas cards instead of the $2500 loss one would normally have incurred by mailing 10,000 people.

The jeweler was delighted after a brief "marketing education" about how a certain percentage of these new-found customers would become lifelong customers. This education is the key to getting the most from deals like this.

Let me share the approach . . .

Few realize the "residual value" of newfound customers. Not all customers will come back again. This will be true even if you give them the best quality, pricing and service. However, a certain percentage of them will come back. In this case, over 2780

> **note** First, you have to understand that most people fail to realize the life-time value of a customer. This is where the Joint Venture associate you wish to approach has to be educated.

Chapter 12

people took the pharmacist up on his offer. The jeweler gave away the lion's share of the front end profit but he will earn much more than most realize.

Here's a hypothetical example:

Assume only 10 percent of those who took advantage of the offer were to return the following year and the average purchase the following year was only $500. The jeweler not only profited from the initial deal but he will earn an additional $70,000 he may have never had if it wasn't for the pharmacist's referral. Jewelry is generally "keystone" pricing (meaning the jewelry sells for approximately a 100% mark-up). If only ten percent of the people return and spend an average of $500 that will bring in an additional $139,000.

At keystone pricing, that's an additional $69,500 profit the jeweler will enjoy from this deal.

This doesn't even take into account the fact that satisfied customers may return year after year, creating profits the jeweler would have never enjoyed without the referral and Joint Venture of the pharmacist. Are you beginning to see the possibilities? They are astronomical!

Deals like these can be made with car dealers, contractors, dentists, restaurants and almost any kind of business you can imagine. The beauty of it is that *this is a win/win deal for everyone* and you get paid for arranging the deals.

Other Approaches

In the example above we used Christmas as a "reason why," but a host of reasons to do deals like these can be created. You may approach the market with reasons like:

> note: I can't think of a single business that couldn't make more money by properly utilizing their customer base by endorsing a quality product or service.

- "We've just discovered the most incredible . . . ."

159

- "We've learned of a secret method . . . ."

- "Since my friend is just getting off the ground, ..."

- "This is the most incredible way for you to . . . ."

- "It's only fair we tell you before the rest of the world learns . . . ."

- "We felt we would be remiss if we didn't get you the first opportunity to try . . . ."

The number of approaches is unlimited!

How do you get these deals?

One of the most successful ways to get deals like these is to approach the target market with a pitch like this:

"If I show you how to properly utilize an asset you are overlooking and make you look like the 'Knight in Shining Armor,' would you be willing to share the new-found profits I make for you at a rate of 50 cents on the dollar?"

There are no hard and fast rules. You should structure the deal in whatever way you must. The above has proven itself to be a great approach especially when you explain you'll guarantee the cost to do the deal and take your profits after the costs are returned. I will fund these kind of deals all day although it is not necessary, as most will "see the light" after a few minutes.

How to insure you get paid?

I use a contract of non-disclosure, stipulating the terms of the arrangement, before I ever share the secret to using this incredible concept.

The rules are not set in granite. You should be as flexible as you need to be to get the deal. It all depends on the size, volume, type of deal, and your involvement in the deal.

Chapter 12

As I said, you may change the amount you charge to share the deal, based on the previously mentioned factors. However, you can earn a very lucrative income using this concept by simply showing business people how to re-deploy their existing assets.

How do I get started?

Getting started is easy. All you have to do is identify the deal and write a letter similar to the one below. Also, be sure you follow up the letter with a phone call. Do not share the intellectual property you have to offer until you have your agreement signed and "in hand" by both or all participating parties.

Here's a sample "door opener" which will ring your phones off the hook:

Dear Store Owner:

My name is Mike Enlow (your name). I am a marketing consultant who specializes in creating immediate additional cash flow at literally no cost to you.

Over the years I've developed a number of intellectual property concepts which have been proven, by using little known and overlooked techniques, to increase cash flow almost immediately.

People from almost every business and industry have been tested, and the concepts I want to share with you work in almost every instance.

I have already taken the liberty to look over your business and am certain I can create a surprisingly large amount of cash for you. I will do so on a strict contingency basis. In fact, since I have already found the perfect deal for you, I will put my money into the marketing of the concept.

I will call you on Tuesday or Thursday to discuss this in greater detail; all I ask is that you call my voice mail, state your company name and specify the day that's best for you so we can get together and get the show on the road.

I do these type deals nationwide. Please call right away so I can fit you into my schedule on the days specified. I can guarantee that you will be blown away and quite surprised by how this new concept can add to your bottom line in a matter of weeks. I do all the work, and you reap the benefits.

Since I am very selective in the clients I pick to share this incredible concept, I must ask you sign an "Intellectual Property Rights Agreement" before I can tell you the details of the deal I have in mind for you.

*Sincerely,
Your Name
Marketing Firm Name*

PS. If the dates I've specified are inconvenient for you, go ahead and call just to let me know you are interested. I'll try to arrange a time that is mutually convenient, since the deal I have in mind for you is very important.

You can be assured that you will get the call. Just set up a voice mail box and be sure to find the matching product or service before you mail the letter.

Chapter 12

How do I know which products will work with the clients I get?

Well, there are no set rules. So many products will work when endorsed by the customer owner. However, you will do much better to "brainstorm" over a prospective client's offer before you make the offer. You should even make a few calls to be sure you can put the offer together. As I said earlier, you need to educate one side regarding the "lifetime value" of gaining new customers in order to get the best deal. You can often get as much as 100% of the profit of the sales made by your endorser by simply explaining this misunderstood marketing principle.

How to get the sweetest deals.

If I were starting from scratch I would seek out product sales companies. These deals are the easiest to get. When you work with attorneys, accountants and others the money trickles in slowly. With product sales, the money comes in over a two or three week period.

Look for those companies that already have an established customer database and, more importantly, have a good, strong relationship with their customers.

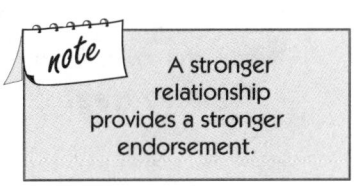

note — A stronger relationship provides a stronger endorsement.

A stronger endorsement provides greater profits. Here are some examples of companies who have a strong relationship with their customers: newsletter publishers, software vendors, chiropractors, radio stations, internet service providers, insurance agents, pharmacists, landscaping experts, etc. They're too numerous to list. Just look for deals where the endorser has a lot of contact with the customer. Preferably, they should at least be in contact with their customers monthly.

How do I decide what to offer in a joint venture?

This can be rather complex depending on the deal. One of the reasons this concept works so well is that the endorser is making the pitch and he or she *already* has the trust of the customer. You should try to find the deal that will yield the greatest possible income. Not everyone who sees their chiropractor would be interested in landscaping, dry cleaning, or radio advertising. So, your offer needs to be one of general appeal to the market. In the case of a chiropractor, I would look for a product which would help people who live in pain or have disabilities. This may be a written report, shark cartilage, or whatever, as long as it meets the demographics of the market. Believe me, no one who has a product or service is going to turn you away as long as the numbers (profit potential numbers) are in their favor.

The world is a big ocean of products and services. You only have to find the one or two products which will yield the greatest possible success to your clients. Not only does this increase your immediate income but it also sets you up to do similar deals with the same clients in the future.

How to maximize your cash flow from every deal

You should look carefully at the easiest client in the world to get—a satisfied and convinced client. This helps you to maximize leverage with every deal you do in order to gain greater and greater income without having to re-sell your concept every time.

For example, if you do a deal with a chiropractor to sell shark cartilage or other pain reliever, the person selling this product also has customers. Almost immediately you can find a deal for the endorsee, which will make his or her cash flow surge—exactly as you've done for the endorser. There are no limits to how far you can take this concept; in fact, it is the single greatest way to leverage.

Chapter 12

Here are a few examples of the kind of deals I would put together right away:

- I would marry car dealers with detail shops who maintain the appearance of cars. Structure the deals so the detail company offers long term (1 year) contracts at a savings of X percentage.

- I would introduce dental patients to companies who sell teeth whitener. Get them on a monthly purchase deal where their credit card is automatically billed and the whitener is automatically shipped as long as the customer wants the product.

- I would marry Internet Service Providers with schools that teach how to get more out of the Internet. Also, I would do deals where I bring software vendors (for an extra profit center) to be introduced to the students each week, month, or for whatever period. There would be a contract for a percentage of the profits when students upgrade the software. This is a trilateral Joint Venture. As you see, the profit potentials are endless!

- Another example would be a Joint Venture between a radio station and a restaurant. I would arrange deals where radio advertising sales representatives receive restaurant meal credits for a percentage of the trade value. This gives them an extra edge in their sales efforts by allowing them to take their clients to dinner. Then, in return, have the radio station give the restaurant the benefit of "cost" advertising. (Radio spots selling for $300 may have a true cost to the radio station of only $100, which gives the restaurant a three to one savings on the radio advertising they are already buying at full price.) You arrange the deal under intellectual property law to receive 20-30% of the "true value" you are rendering to the restaurant.

- I would arrange deals where software vendors share lists and make offers to each other's customer base. Of course, I would take my

165

piece of the pie. This is a very lucrative area, especially if you arrange the deal where you continue to get a percentage of upgrades, etc.

Summary

I hope you are beginning to see that this is an untapped area of marketing where you, as a consultant, can cash in on others' lack of observation or understanding while doing a noble win/win service to the business community.

I've just given you the blueprint to your financial independence. If you want to learn how to turbo-leverage these concepts immediately, I strongly suggest that you join our new "Masters of Marketing Inner Circle" program. As a member, you will receive the equivalent of a marketing Ph.D. (and then some). Plus, you'll receive a unique tool that I've spent close to $100,000 developing that will allow you to have over 50 of the world's greatest marketing minds at your fingertips to answer virtually any marketing question you may have.

Michael Enlow

This Joint Venture report has been included here with permission from Michael E. Enlow. The intellectual property herein is the property of Michael E. Enlow, and *may not* be distributed to third parties, as it is as well copyrighted under the laws of the United States and many foreign country treatises. © 1996-2000 Michael E. Enlow. All Rights Reserved.

There's really nothing more I can say about joint venture marketing—Mike's article was far more than I could have contributed myself. For many of you, the above article will be all you need to know about joint ventures.

However, if you want to learn even more about this method, go to his URL to download his 14-chapter ebook about joint ventures and internet marketing:

http://www.enlowcircle.com/

Chapter 12

If you're really serious, you should join Mike's "Inner Circle." Once you've joined, you will be able to download sample contracts and letters, audio and video training, question/answer transcripts, and lots more about this and other marketing-related topics.

Here's the link again:

http://www.enlowcircle.com/go/1050

(affiliate link)

Legal resources

13

Legal resources

There are some great legal resources available online. Software, free legal forms, research sites, and even legal services—it's all here. On the next page I have included an article about the relatively new "COPPA" law and what you should be doing to be sure you're in compliance with it.

Legal Forms

Free:

http://www.MadeE-Z.com

http://www.ilrg.com/forms

http://www.lectlaw.com/formb.htm

http://www.legaldocs.com
[Fill in the blank document generator]

http://www.allaboutforms.com

http://www.legalresource.com/legalforms.htm

http://www.allbusiness.com/form_docs/forms_index.asp

Online Business Resources Made E-Z

For Pay:

> http://www.MadeE-Z.com
>
> http://www.contractcentral.com
>
> http://www.uslegalforms.com
>
> http://www.quickforms.net (Create Online)
>
> http://www.legaldocs.com (Create Online)

Software:

> http://www.Made-E-Z.com
>
> http://www.contractcentral.com
>
> http://www.lawyerware.com/

Other Legal Sites:

> http://www.startpage.com/html/law.html
> (Directory of Law Links)
>
> http://www.nolo.com/
> (Self help, software, Q&A, etc.)
>
> http://www.lawguru.com/
> (Self help, free answers to legal questions, more)
>
> http://www.itislaw.com
> [Law Library (case law database, $49.95/month)]

Chapter 13

Trademark information:

http://www.marksonline.com

http://www.trademark.com

Miscellaneous:

I thought this was a service worthy of mention here. In their own words, FirstUse.com allows you to "Digitally Fingerprint, Timestamp, and Register any file to strengthen legal documentation and create a tamperproof audit trail for personal or business records, copyrights, patents, trademarks, and trade secrets."

http://www.firstuse.com/ms.htm

Privacy Statement Generators. More and more people expect you to have (and actively look for) a privacy statement on your web site. These tools help you create a statement customized to your own unique requirements.

http://www.etrust.com/wizard

http://www.the-dma.org/library/privacy/creating.shtml

COPPA Article

Most people don't even know what the COPPA law is, and many that do know what it is do not have a full understanding of how they might be in violation of it. Please read this article carefully—you might be surprised to learn that you are required to be in compliance!

NEW U.S. LAW HAS WIDE IMPACT ON THE INTERNET

By Michael Martinez

Online interactions with children

Not very long ago a teenager asked me for advice on how to create a web site. We discussed her interests and what she thought she could do, and then I made some suggestions on how to create the content for a unique web site.

When the girl was wrapping up her work, she asked me how to create the actual pages. In other words, she did not already have web space to use. At that point, I told her a little more about myself and advised her to sit down and discuss what she wanted to do with her parents or a teacher at school, and to make sure they understood she had been in communication with me about this project.

In order to help her create a web site, I would either have to ask her for private information such as her name and address, or at least instruct her in how to give this information to a web-hosting service. I have no right to solicit such information from underage people. Nor should I be advising them to give out that information to other people. This last part of our exchange occurred only a few days after I had become aware of the Children's Online Privacy Protection Act of 1998.

Act took effect April 22, 2000

This law, passed in October 1998, took effect on April 21, 2000. The Federal Trade Commission has been authorized by Congress to administer the law, and accordingly the FTC solicited input from responsible organizations and the public last year in order to put the final rule into proper form. Unfortunately, many other people and I knew nothing about this process, and

Chapter 13

the final rule has been implemented without any input from a lot of us. In fact, barely more than 140 individuals and organizations provided comments on a rule which will effect millions of people. For the children's sake, we have to hope it is a well-written rule, but there are some open issues.

To whom does it apply?

One of the chief concerns over this law is to whom it applies. The United States has no jurisdiction over the Internet outside its borders. Some people feel the law may put American businesses into a poorly competitive position. Perhaps, but big business usually finds a way to survive. And other countries may enact similar laws in the near future. The Internet is already governed by international treaty in some areas such as copyright, trademark, libel, and pornography. The international community is slowly but surely building up a framework of law that will apply to everyone or nearly everyone using the Internet.

The new law, known as COPPA, was designed to govern the practices of commercial web sites that interact with children. But someone somewhere in the process extended the law's coverage to include *any* service that interacts with children. This broader application is of particular interest to non-commercial webmasters for several reasons.

Kids and private information

First of all, many of us have children to protect. Even if they are not our own, we might find ourselves in positions of responsibility. A few months ago I helped my 8-year-old niece register for Zoog Disney. It is a big thing with kids, but Zoog required parental consent for the registration. Once we got that taken care of, my niece could do all sorts of things on the Zoog site. I stepped away from the computer for a few minutes and when I came back I found she had a credit card sitting on the keyboard and she was about to order some merchandise.

Children are not precocious when it comes to buying things on the Internet. Keeping the credit cards out of their hands is only one aspect of being responsible for them on the Internet. What about those Whizkid

175

webmasters who set up the fantastic web sites? Where do they get the web space? Some are using Mom and Dad's accounts, but many young people are signing up with free web space providers. How many parents are actually involved in these web contracts? Do they know what information their children are giving out, or what services their children are signing up for?

Parents may not be aware that kids can now download and install (on their own PCs) software from free Internet Service Providers such as *NetZero*, *Excite*, and *Alta Vista*. They do not have to use Mom and Dad's accounts any more, even though these ISP's may be trying to restrict access only to adults. What is to prevent a determined child from clicking on the "Yes, I am 18 or older" button? Nothing.

ON-LINE SERVICES INCLUDE CHAT ROOMS AND MESSAGE BOARDS

But where the online community of webmasters becomes directly concerned with the privacy of children is the provision under COPPA for including "online services" in the target population which must comply with this law. An online service includes a chat room or message board. The FTC is not talking about *America Online*. They are talking about specific services that any webmaster can install on his or her site: chat rooms and message boards. Also, if you simply run a newsletter, you, too, may have to comply with the law.

The FTC rule says:

If you operate a commercial web site or an online service directed to children under 13 that collects personal information from children, or if you operate a general audience web site and have actual knowledge that it collects personal information from children, you must comply with the *Children's Online Privacy Protection Act.*

Chapter 13

How many of us are directing our chat rooms and message boards to the under 13 crowd? The FTC has decided they will use the following criteria for determining who is and who is not targeting children:

> To determine whether a web site is directed to children, the FTC will consider several factors, including the subject matter, visual or audio content, the age of models on the site, language, whether advertising on the web site is directed to children, information regarding the age of the actual or intended audience, and whether a site uses animated characters or other child-oriented features.

Many non-commercial web sites are devoted to obviously mature themes. It may, perhaps, be a good idea for the webmasters to put up a note indicating children should not browse the site, but you need to be careful about what advertising you put on your site. If you are a member of an affiliate or associate program (some online merchants use these terms in different ways), you may have some direct links with graphics which could give the impression you are targeting children. Web sites which promote services or products which could appeal to children are in a gray area.

Not so gray areas?

Web sites with content about actors and actresses who have appeared in children's television shows and movies, or about children's activities, or which provide information of an encyclopedic nature on a level children can easily understand will probably be perceived as directing their content toward children. Message boards or chats devoted to similar topics will further draw such web sites out of the gray area into required compliance.

Reviews of movies and books directed at children, or even just bibliographies which children might use for school projects, also propel non-commercial web sites into the arena of interacting with children. Web sites which carry the popular *AskJeeves* for Kids search box or similar services are clearly targeting children.

177

Of course, just because you have got referral links on your web site does not mean you are required to comply with the law. The question comes down to whether you are initiating an ongoing communication with your visitors, and if you know whether these visitors (or some of them) are children under the age of 13. If you are not hosting chat services, message boards, and newsletters, are you in the clear? Maybe. What about that guest book you have got on your site? Does it not ask for names and email addresses? Is it not making that information available to third parties? Will COPPA be the death of the guest book tradition that many perfectly innocent web sites have employed for years?

What is private information?

This is what the FTC regards to be private information as defined by COPPA:

The Children's Online Privacy Protection Act and Rule apply to individually identifiable information about a child that is collected online, such as full name, home address, email address, telephone number or any other information that would allow someone to identify or contact the child. The Act and Rule also cover other types of information—for example, hobbies, interests and information collected through cookies or other types of tracking mechanisms—when they are tied to individually identifiable information.

If a child contacts you on his or her own initiative, you are probably safe as long as the contact is for a one-time purpose. The FTC ruling speaks of homework questions, but there are plenty of other innocent exchanges that happen. We occasionally receive email from children who want to know how to contact members of the television shows we have devoted web space to. Sometimes children ask us for help in finding things on the web. I may think twice about giving out that kind of advice in the future. But these kinds of contacts are regarded as reasonable exclusions.

However, any webmaster who must otherwise comply with the law is expected to immediately delete any private information (including email addresses) they acquire from these exchanges once they are finished. So much for keeping a record of your past emails. If you have to go hunting for something to give advice to a child once, you will have to find some way of preserving the results of your search without violating the child's privacy, or else go hunting again if you are ever asked the same question twice.

Now parents who volunteer their time and resources to help with local school projects need to think twice about how they implement the web sites. And what about teachers who put up web sites for their classes? If they are not interacting with the children they should be fine, but if they are soliciting comments from children (even members of their own classes), what measures do they need to take to comply with the law? If they confine their web interaction to official school domains, compliance may be covered by whatever the school administrators implement, but teachers may have to work more closely with their online admins to ensure compliance.

Non-commercial sites impacted

Like me with my domain, Xenite.Org, many non-commercial webmasters create several mini-web sites within one large web site. My content covers Xena, Hercules, Edgar Rice Burroughs, J.R.R. Tolkien, Andre Norton, Farscape, Sir Arthur Conan Doyle's *The Lost World* (and that includes the book, the movies, and the television series), and more. I am not going to be able to duck the "mass appeal" criterion, and many other SF & F webmasters will find themselves in the same boat as me. It is not just the commercial webmastering community that needs to worry about complying with this law. Even the typical homepage may fall under the law's jurisdiction, as most people have more than one interest. A homepage with essays and link lists about books, movies, hobbies, activities, their local communities, and more may be regarded as having mass appeal.

A directory, no matter how specialized, is certainly intended for a large audience and not just friends and family. Web resource sites, free and cool stuff sites, award-program sites, and sites which promote community activism all fall into the category of non-commercial sites which are impacted by the law.

But what will happen if we non-commercial webmasters do not try to comply? Only time will tell, but given that there are millions of web sites devoted to all manner of interests and activities with "mass appeal" (e.g., horses, cooking, consumer rights, science, history, literature, etc.) it appears that the web Content Monitors will not be knocking on many peoples' doors right away. The law will be reviewed in two years and we will see where we go from there.

Policing the Act

It will be a largely self-regulating effort and doubtless people will be keeping an eye on large commercial kids' sites like Disney.Com, Ty.Com, CartoonNetwork.Com, et. al. to see what standards they adopt. Privacy and legal industry groups will be consulted and looked to to help define these self-regulating standards. But the final question two years from now will be, have we all done enough?

> **note** The business community has, for this first two-year period, been given an opportunity to set up its own industry standards for compliance.

What the websites can do

What, specifically, does the law require of web sites which must comply with its requirements? You have to post a privacy policy on your site, and you must link to it in any page which initiates some sort of ongoing relationship (commercial, discussion, or informative) with your visitors. The policy must state your procedure for verifying parental permission to conduct ongoing relationships with children.

There are several options for doing this, but the requirements are more stringent for sites that sell products or services to children. Not sites that are affiliates or associates of online resellers, mind you. The book stores, CD stores, and other online retailers are the people collecting the information and distributing the merchandise. But you may need to make clear in *your* privacy

Chapter 13

policy that *you* are *not* collecting this information, that it does not pass through your hands, and that you are not responsible for its uses.

The privacy policy requirement also stipulates that the "operators" of the web site or online service must make their offline contact information (name, postal address, and telephone number) available to parents. This is necessary for ensuring that children do not have an easy opportunity to fake a parent's approval. Not everyone is required to give out this information.

The FTC says:

> *To determine whether an entity is an "operator" with respect to information collected at a site, the FTC will consider who owns and controls the information; who pays for the collection and maintenance of the information; what the pre-existing contractual relationships are in connection with the information; and what role the web site plays in collecting or maintaining the information.*

First of all, if you have volunteers or employees helping with your web site, or if you are paying people to help with your web site, they are off the hook (as far as your web site goes). Secondly, if you are using a third-party service, or are referring people to online retailers for commissions, such that you are not directly collecting or using the private information, you are off the hook. An organization which is a legal entity can publish its office address, but individuals operating their own web sites will have to provide some very personal information.

> **note** — If you control the information that a third-party service acquires in the process of maintaining your service, you may become liable under the law. You are responsible for the information that you collect and use, regardless of whether you are selling anything.

If you are running your own mailing lists, message boards, chat rooms, or distributing your own newsletters, you are the "operator." If instead of running your own services

181

you sign up with EZBoard or InsideTheweb, or Onelist or Topica, you should be in the clear, unless they give you access to the personal information that their registrants provide to them. A child's privacy is not vulnerable just through a commercial web site. And the purpose of the law is to protect children's private information, not to regulate commerce.

Problems with the law

Did the lawmakers and the people at the Federal Trade Commission stop to consider that non-commercial webmasters who have to comply with this law are exposing their own private information? As a domain name registrant I have entered my personal information into a publicly accessible database. But what about people who do not register their own domains? Is it trivial to require them (many of whom are women who have taken measures to protect their own privacy) to post their full names, addresses, and telephone numbers on their web sites just because they are running message boards or chat rooms?

I have questioned some people about the freeware that is available on the web. It appears that the originators of these scripts are not going to assume the burden of ensuring that a webmaster is in compliance with the law. If you download and install any free version of a message board or mailing list script, you cannot look to the software to cover you. There may be registration features which give you control over who is able to post information to the board and how much personal information is disclosed, but you must still take measures to ensure that either your content excludes you from coverage under the law or that you have set up a procedure for acquiring parental permission for the child who makes use of your services.

Even commercial versions of these kinds of applications will not offer any guarantees of compliance. No software provider can assume that kind of liability.

Chapter 13

If you are running your own CGI applications now, and you are sure you are collecting information from children that is not protected, you should make some changes, but do not get your hopes up about finding a miracle application. Adding a registration requirement to your services will slightly inconvenience your communities, but the kids might just go elsewhere, since larger, commercial sites already require registration and soon will all require parental verification. And they also have many more goodies than the local webmaster can provide. The law provides a few conditions where prior parental consent is not required for collecting information, but there are conditions attached (see the links at the end of the article for further details on such provisions).

> **note** It is the webmaster's responsibility alone to ensure the web site is in compliance with the law.

Mass appeal test

It is important to know whether your content has "mass appeal," or if it appeals to children. There are already some guidelines available for determining if a web site is appropriate for children. You can check out the standards published by the Internet Content Rating Service. Their site includes a table that shows what ratings are applied to what content. At the very least, if you can determine that your content is inappropriate for children, you can then say so on your web site (if you feel that would not be harmful to the way your site is perceived).

> **note** In most cases we do not want to put "Adults only" on our web sites. But if you want to exclude your site from compliance with COPPA you will need to ensure it does not look like it is intended for children.

The "mass appeal" rule is harder to cope with. At Xenite.Org, for example, we do not forbid the use of profanity on our message boards, but we strongly discourage it. We insist our discussion communities be civil

183

and polite to one another. That provision was created for purely personal reasons. I wanted flame-free communities. But parents do not mind letting their kids browse our boards in part because we maintain a civil atmosphere. Many other message board communities have similar guidelines, and they are also visited by people of all ages.

Would <u>Xenite.Org</u> be rated "Kid Safe"? Probably not quite, but we would get a pretty good rating nonetheless. But if we put "Kid Safe" on our web pages we are all but saying we intend to provide content for children and therefore we need to comply with the law. Up until now it was a great thing to be able to say your site is "Kid Safe." Now you need to think twice. If you do not get the "Kid Safe" rating, where does that leave you? Kids may still come and sign your guest book, sign up for your newsletter, join your message board, and enter your chat area. But if you put "For adults only" on your site, then you are giving a much different and in most cases the wrong impression. We may need a new, neutral content rating.

Checking liability

If you currently use remotely hosted applications, you should review the application providers' terms of service agreements and privacy policies. If these documents have not been updated to show these services are aware of the law, then you should contact the service providers. Try to get some clear idea of who they feel is responsible for complying with the law. If they say *they* and *they* alone are, do not worry about it. If, however, the application providers you are using suggest you may also be liable (because you have access to the private information), then you should consider what you can do to either minimize your obligations under the law or to live up to them.

Children are everyone's responsibility

Inevitably, if we as webmasters, parents, guardians, and employees of businesses which operate commercial web sites or online services shirk the moral obligation to help ensure this law becomes effective, we will share in

Chapter 13

the burden of its failure and whatever consequences that failure brings, such as more stringent rules and regulations further down the road. But more importantly, we are leaving it to someone else to protect the children. An ounce of prevention is worth a pound of cure. That is the philosophy behind this law.

> **note** It may not take much for the majority of us to help ensure the kids' privacy is protected. But we are entering a new era of greater responsibility for everyone, and regardless of whether you feel the law is well-designed, it is here. Let us deal with it as best we can.

For further reading

For further reading, the following web sites provide detailed and explicit information on the *Children's Online Privacy Protection Act:*

How To Comply With The Children's Online Privacy Protection Rule:

http://www.ftc.gov/bcp/conline/pubs/buspubs/coppa.htm

Children's Online Privacy Protection Act of 1998:

http://www.ftc.gov/opa/1999/9910/childfinal.htm

Center for Media Education's COPPA resources:

http://www.cme.org/

Kid's Privacy.Org:

http://www.kidsprivacy.org/

Internet Content Rating Association:

http://www.icra.org/

Internet Law Journal article on COPPA:

http://www.internetlawjournal.com/content/ecomarticle11159901.htm

Zoog Disney is a trademark of Disney Enterprises, Inc.

Onelist is a trademark of eGroups, Inc.

Ty is a trademark of Ty, Inc.

Article by Michael Martinez, michael@xenite.org

http://www.xenite.Org

Miscellaneous

14

14

Miscellaneous

There are a number of topics with too few resources to justify a section of their own, but they are still very useful to the business owner. In fact, sometimes I get more out of the "miscellaneous" section of a resource guide than any other section! Here they are in no particular order.

Free Internet access

Though I believe you should have an account with a local internet service provider, these ad-supported services can be a real lifesaver when your primary service is down or when you're traveling. There are others besides these, but these are the main three, and the only ones I've heard enough about to include them here:

Juno: http://www.juno.com

Net Zero: http://www.netzero.com

BlueLight: http://www.bluelight.com

Virtual assistants

Need help with your everyday office tasks? You may be able to use a "virtual assistant." These are real people (not a software program) who "telecommute"—you communicate with them via phone, email, and fax.

If you're spending too much time with the menial everyday tasks, think about hiring a virtual assistant (at least on a part-time basis). You shouldn't be neglecting your promotion and development because of these things!

http://www.va4hire.com

Background checks

Need to verify someone's education? How about checking their employment history? This outfit will supply these reports and others (including a felony report and credit report).

http://www.crimeassure.com

Magic-floppy technique

This is more appropriate to a book on marketing techniques, but I've wanted to share it ever since I published my first book (I found out about this technique just after publication).

I first heard about this technique from Don Alm (http://www.pjbux.com), and later from Michael Ross (http://www.ozemail.com.au/~miros/index.htm). This is a method both of these men have used to achieve very high response rates to their sales letters (sent via snail-mail).

Basically what they do is place a classified or small display advertisement in a local print publication (i.e. the local paper or ad magazine). When people respond to the advertisement, they send out a sales letter—and a floppy disk. The sales letter expounds on the value of the information they are selling and tells the prospect he already has the information; it's on the floppy disk—but it has been encrypted. All they need to do is call in to get the unlock code and they can start using the material immediately.

It works great, because curiosity just breaks the prospect down. He knows he can have all the answers to his questions in a matter of minutes—all he has to do is call in with his credit card number. I suppose it's a lot like Shareware.

Chapter 14

Anyway, there are a number of software programs to create an encrypted, self-executing file. By that I mean all the person has to do is double-click on the file—it will ask for the unlock code and if they enter the right code, it will decrypt the file. Here are two pieces of software to do this:

Norton Secret Stuff: http://www.download.com (Free)

WinZip: http://www.winzip.com

Barter

I haven't tried this yet, but I've heard some very good things about the potentials of bartering. It seems to me that a barter exchange member would be more apt to buy my products if he could use "barter dollars" he had obtained by bartering some of his surplus inventory—so I'd like to try mailing an offer to a list of exchange members.

It's almost like an "easy come, easy go" attitude. If he hadn't bartered it, he'd most likely have had to throw it out, liquidate it for pennies on the dollar, or give it away as a charitable contribution. Definitely worth a look!

http://www.ubarter.com

http://tnc.ware.net/bxi/index.html (BXI)

Content conversion

These utilities allow you to convert your documents to HTML and PDF.

EasyDoc converts HTML documents to Adobe Acrobat PDF files. The software is free, and you can purchase product support if you need to.

http://www.easysw.com/htmldoc/

Gohtm.com is an online service for converting several different document formats to HTML. This includes PDF files, RTF ("Rich Text") files, Microsoft Word and Excel files, and others. It's free, but they add their own banner to the bottom of each page.

http://www.gohtm.com

ClicktoConvert software converts documents to HTML. It's cost was $149 at the time of printing this guide, but it has some advanced features not offered by Gohtm—and nothing gets added to your documents.

http://www.clicktoconvert.com

Copywriters

You have three choices:

1) Continue writing so-so copy and continue getting so-so (or worse) results.

2) Learn to write great copy, apply your knowledge, and reap the rewards.

3) Shell out some bucks and let a professional copywriter worry about it.

note: Good copywriting makes all the difference between a campaign that barely breaks even (or loses money) and one that is wildly successful.

#1 is for people who aren't serious about their business.

#2 is for people who are serious about their business, want to be involved in and understand copywriting, and have the time to learn to do it right.

#3 is for people who are serious about their business but don't have the time to learn and implement this aspect of it for themselves.

Chapter 14

If you want to learn to do it yourself, there are many good books that will help you (but no book is a substitute for experience). I have listed several of these books in the "Copywriting" section of the appendix.

If you want to hire someone to do your copywriting for you, here are a few highly recommended copywriters:

Nan Yielding: http://www.writing-etc.com

Linda Caroll: http://www.lindacaroll.com

Trevor Levine: levine@marketingexperts.com

Scott Smith: scott@infowriters.com

Drew Eric Whitman: drdirect@adsurgeon.com

Joe Robson: http://www.adcopywriting.com

Anthony Blake: ablake@ablake.com

Dr. Kevin Nunley: http://www.drnunley.com

Denny Hatch: http://methodmarketing.com/about.html

Rene Gnam: http://www.renegnam.com

Text editors

Every now and then I find someone on the discussion boards I frequent asking about "text editors." As a programmer I use text editors extensively. I'm not sure how many people reading this guide are in need of a text editor (I usually associate such things with technical work), but if you are in need of a good one, here are some great choices:

This is the one I use, and I'm practically in love with it. Very powerful with HEX mode, macro capabilities, search/replace across all open files or all files in a directory, FTP upload functions built in, and lots more. A fine piece of software if ever there was one!

UltraEdit: http://www.ultraedit.com

Though I haven't used these others, they have been highly recommended by people whose opinions I respect, so I'm confident they're good packages:

Boxer: http://www.boxersoftware.com

extPad: http://www.textpad.com

NoteTab: http://www.notetab.com

Download sites

The number of freely available software programs is exploding. Just about any kind of software you need can be obtained at one of the below download sites. Generally, the software is limited in some fashion unless/until you pay a registration fee, but there are a surprising number of very good totally free packages as well. These are great places to research "the hottest software," too!

TuCows: http://www.tucows.com

Download.com: http://www.download.com

Jumbo: http://www.jumbo.com

ZDNet: http://www.zdnet.com/downloads

Chapter 14

Online printing / duplication services

Generally I recommend you work with local sources for this kind of thing, as you have more control over the situation that way—you can inspect the finished products before accepting them. However, sometimes you'll get better pricing through some of these online sources, which is great until you have a problem with the quality.

Printing:

http://www.iprint.com

http://www.printbuyer.com

http://www.noosh.com

http://www.printingforless.com

http://www.kinkos.com

And don't forget about Mimeo.com—I mentioned them earlier. If you need *fast* printing and delivery (to your customer) of single quantities, nobody offers greater convenience.

http://www.mimeo.com

Video / CDROM / Cassette duplication:

IMS Video Dist: Contact Mark Miller 888-828-3873

Recording Products: http://www.recordingproducts.com

Karol Media: http://www.karolmedia.com

Dicobe Tapes: http://www.dicobe.com/

NorthStar Video   818-908-0894 (Fax 818-904-9004)

Post card marketing

These companies will help you design your postcard marketing pieces, then they'll print and mail them for you.

I've worked directly with Markus Allen at mailshopusa.com before and feel pretty good about recommending his service. Be sure to grab his free postcard marketing "e-report" from his website.

> http://www.mailshopusa.com

I haven't worked with this company before, but I sure do get their postcards a lot—they obviously practice what they preach, and it must be working for them.

> http://www.postcardpower.com

Privacy

Here are a few sites to visit if you're concerned with your own privacy on the internet.

ZixMail: Secure document delivery, private email and message tracking service that enables Internet users worldwide to easily send and receive encrypted and digitally signed communications using their existing email systems and addresses.

> http://www.zixmail.com

GuardLock: Your private information is available on the Internet and through many traditional information brokers. GuardLock protects your privacy by removing your information from public access.

> http://www.guardlock.com

Chapter 14

Shop (and actually buy things) anonymously online. Great idea, allows you to use the number they assign you as a credit card (MasterCard) number.

http://www.privatebuy.com

Viral marketing

The only reason I decided to include this short discussion about "viral marketing" is because I've seen so many self-proclaimed "marketing experts" evangelizing this method of marketing on the internet—and then incorrectly explaining it.

> **note** Some people equate the giving away of your own ebook to viral marketing—but there's a subtle (but very important) qualifier that must be met for this to be true.

Viral marketing is a service or product you provide that promotes itself when it is used. Does an ebook do this? Not unless somewhere in the ebook (preferably at the top or bottom of each page) you have a link saying "Click here to send this ebook to a friend" or something similar. That's even a weak example.

Here are some much *better* examples of *real* viral marketing:

"Pass this on." Go to this site to find a "cartoon" page you might want to show your friends. You submit their email address, and they receive an email saying "check this out" or something similar. They, of course, must come to the site (the same one you visited) to view the humorous cartoon.

In a very short period of time, this site has risen to the #24 position (as of this writing) in the list of most visited web sites. The owner can monetize this huge amount of traffic with banner advertising, affiliate programs, or "cost per action" deals (see advertising section for details).

197

http://www.passthison.com

Virtual Card sites. Go to a virtual card site such as "Blue Mountain Arts," choose an appropriate picture, sound clip, and message, and send it to a friend. When they get an email notification, they click on a link and view your card—and they're invited to send you a card in reply.

http://www.bluemountainarts.com

ICQ was discussed in the "Communications" section. It allows you to send "instant messages" to anyone else who has it installed on their computer. If you want to send someone an ICQ message and they don't have ICQ, you are invited to fill out a form—the submission of which will send an email to this friend inviting them to download and install the ICQ program.

http://www.icq.com

Online business web sites

Some of these are so obvious, and that's exactly why many people never think of them.

http://www.inc.com

http://entrepreneur.com

http://www.businessweek.com

http://www.successmagazine.com

http://www.allbusiness.com

http://www.workz.com

http://www.eboz.com

Chapter 14

Web sites ranked

These sites allow you to see who the rising online stars are, measured by popularity.

http://www.hitbox.com

http://www.100hot.com

Online payment methods 15

15

Online payment methods

As a seller of "real-time credit card processing" enabled software, I have observed that many business owners don't quite understand how all the pieces fit. Some of you "Internet business savvy" people may know all this already, so feel free to skip ahead.

Implementing an "E-Commerce" site (a web site where you take credit card orders) generally requires these four things:

1) A web site hosting service.

2) A "secure" ordering page.

3) A merchant account.

4) A payment processing service.

Web site hosting service

A web site hosting service is a company that "rents" space and "bandwidth" (data transfer) on their internet servers to you. If you had a lot of money and an in-house technical staff, you could get your own web server with a leased data line, but most of us are better off just using a reliable web hosting company. I discuss web hosting services in greater detail in the section on web site resources.

Secure order form

A secure order form is required if you want your customers to feel comfortable sending their personal information (address, credit card number, etc). There's a lot of misinformation about just what a secure order form is. The HTML file itself is not any different from any other "regular" HTML file. (HTML is the "markup language" used to make web pages.).

What *is* different is how the data is transferred from your computer to the web server. If you enter information into a "secure" order form and then "send" it, your web browser encrypts the data before sending it to the web server. Note there's nothing unique about the file itself. The security comes from how the data is sent back and forth, not from any characteristics of the file.

Similarly, when you enter a "secure" URL (one that starts with "https" instead of "http") into your browser location window, the web server will encrypt the contents of that requested page before sending it to your computer. Your browser will then decrypt that information in order to show you the page.

In order to deliver your order form via a "secure" connection, you must have a SSL (secure socket layer) certificate from one of the digital certificate services or you can often use the secure certificate of your web hosting company. Ask your web hosting company for details about these two options.

Merchant account

A merchant account is an account you have with a bank. With a merchant account, you can accept credit card payments. You process the payments via a "card swipe" (hardware) terminal, a software terminal program on your computer, or an "online" terminal provided by a processing service.

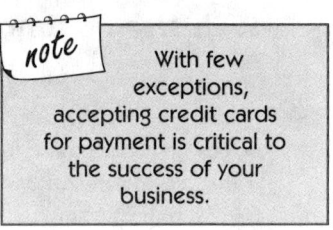

> **note** With few exceptions, accepting credit cards for payment is critical to the success of your business.

204

Chapter 15

People love to use plastic and will order things with their credit cards that they might not purchase otherwise. Virtually all direct marketing impulse spending is done with a credit card, so you must have this capability to compete—and possibly just to survive.

Here's a quote from something I read online:

Unless you have been in business for 2 years with a Dunn and Bradstreet referral, two years of tax returns, an "A paper" credit rating, and probably several other hoops, you will have very little chance, if any at all, of getting Merchant Account Software for Major Credit Card acceptance for your business or individual use.

All I can say to that is baloney. The people who are responsible for the above statement were trying to make small business owners believe the only way they were going to get a credit card merchant account was through this company—at an outrageous cost of $1800. Just about anyone with decent credit can get a merchant account—even if you have bad credit there are ways around it. If for some reason you just can't get your own merchant account, take heart. There are other ways you can cash in on the plastic craze. In fact, there are actually some advantages to some of the alternatives.

The first place you should attempt to get a merchant account is your local bank. You may be surprised to find they welcome your merchant account business, and you'll never know until you try. If that doesn't pan out, and if you have a "Costco" nearby, signup for their "Executive Business Membership," which includes very reasonably priced credit card merchant services.

No Costco nearby? No problem.

On the following two pages you will find a list of some of the companies who will work with you to get your own merchant account. I evaluated a number of other companies as well, but eliminated them for various reasons (chief of which is their startup cost).

Several of these companies do work with international merchants, but rates for international merchants are higher than those listed in this table.

Some merchant account providers claim they work with international merchants, but they require U.S. incorporation. Maybe I'm missing something, but that doesn't sound like an international account anymore—so I put "no" in their "international" column.

An outfit called "ProPay" is worth special mention (http://propay.com). They make it extremely easy to get a merchant account (At least for U.S. companies. I'm not sure if they work with international merchants or not). They normally process your online application in 24 hours, and there's no application fee.

Now, there is a caveat. With ProPay you are only allowed $1000 per month in merchant account transactions, and each order is limited to a maximum of $250. You can raise these limits to $2000/$300 and $3000/$500 by "pre-funding" your account.

Obviously, this isn't for everyone, but for some people it will be the easiest way by far to get what they need.

Payment processing service

Finally, a payment processing service is a company with the ability to clear credit card transactions through the various credit card companies (Visa, Mastercard, etc). On the Internet these are often referred to as "real-time" services, meaning the credit card is checked and approved (or rejected) immediately, and the customer knows right away if the charge was approved or denied.

If the charge is approved, the order process continues to completion, and an email receipt is usually sent to the customer and to the business owner.

Chapter 15

Company	URL	APP	HW / SW	MSF	MM	CBF	INTL?	RTS
2CheckOut.com Inc.	http://www.2checkout.com	0	0 / 0	0	0	25	yes	yes
Advantage Bankcard Services	http://www.creditcardsaccept.com	0	235 / 195	895	15	15	no	A
Advantage Merchant Services	http://www.creditcardprocessor.com	0	23900 / 14900	10	0	15	yes	yes
AIS Media Corporation	http://www.aismedia.com	0	0 / 35	10	25	15	no	yes
Bancard E-CommerceSolutions	http://www.ecommwebsolutions.com	0	95 / 95	10	20	15	no	yes
Bancard Technologies	http://www.bancardtechnologies.com	0	2599 / 2299	10	25	0	no	A
Bankcard	http://www.merchantbankcard.com	115	0 / 165	9	25	15	No	Yes
BankCard & Check Processing	http://www.creativepaymentsystems.com	0	24.95 / 19.95	10	25	15	yes	yes
BankCard Solutions	http://www.bankcardsolutions.com	0	16 / 20	5	0	15	No	A,C
BerryHill Financial	http://www.berryhillfinancial.com	75	0 / 17.99	12.5	20	25	No	A,S
Capital Bankcard	http://www.merchantwarehouse.com	0	180 / 0	10	0	10	Yes	A,C,P,M
Credit Payment Services	http://www.edpcc.com	0	0 / 0	5	0	20	yes	yes
CardReady of West LA	http://www.chargewest.com	99	0 / 0	10	25	20	no	yes
Cardservice Express Services	http://www.cardserviceexpress.com	0	1999 / 0	10	15	15	no	yes
Cardservice-BSDC	http://www.card-payment.com	0	0 / 0	5	15	15	no	A,L
Century Resources Inc.	http://www.accept-visa.com	0	0 / 0	10	25	10	no	A
Charge.Com Merchant Services	http://www.charge.com	0	0 / 195	10	25	25	yes	yes
Community Bankers	http://www.merchantprocessing.com	0	15 / 0	0	0	0	no	yes
Credit Card Processing Services	http://www.mcvisa.com	0	0 / 0	5	0	10	yes	A,C,P
Credit Card Solutions	http://www.creditcardsolutions.net	0	1990 / 2590	25 (*)	0	15	Yes	Yes
Creditcardman.com	http://www.creditcardman.com	0	0 / 0	10	25	15	no	yes
Creditcards.com	http://www.creditcards.com	50	39 / 39	10	25	25	yes	yes
Cross Country Bank	http://www.crosscountrybank.com	50	0 / 0	25	0	25	no	NDC
CyberAuthorize.com	http://www.cyberauthorize.com	0	0 / 0	10	10	10	no	A,S,S,I
Delaware Merchant Services	http://www.demerchantservices.com	50	0 / 0	5	10	20	yes	A,S
E-Commerce Exchange	http://www.ecommerceapproved.com	50	0 / 0	10	25	15	yes	yes
Ecxweb	http://www.ecxweb.com	0	39 / 39	10	15	15	yes	yes
Electronic Payment Processing	http://www.epp-inc.com	0	0 / 0	10	0	0	no	yes
Electronic Transfer, Inc.	http://www.electronictransfer.com	0	0 / 35	95	15	15	yes	yes
Elite Payment Solutions	http://www.elitepaymentsolutions.com	50	150 / 150	10	15	15	no	yes
Emerald Coast Services	http://www.ez-creditcard.com	75	0 / 0	125	20	15	no	yes
EpaymentSource.com	http://www.epaymentsource.com	0	3995 / 3995	10	20	15	no	yes

207

Online Business Resources Made E-Z

Company	URL	APP	HW / SW	MSF	MM	CBF	INTL?	RTS
EZ Merchant Accounts	http://www.ezmerchantaccounts.com	0	0 / 0	95	25	20	no	Yes
First National BankCard	http://www.merchantbankcard.com	115	0 / 165	9	25	35	no	yes
For Him Processing	http://www.fhp2000.com	45	0 / 250	8	0	15	no	yes
Front Line Processing	http://www.frontlineprocessing.com	0	500 / 0	10	25	30	No	Yes
Global Card Service	http://www.1stglobalcardservice.com	95	0 / 0	10	20	15	no	yes
GORealtime.com	http://www.gorealtime.com	0	0 / 0	10	0	0	no	yes
GUAR	http://www.amsfirst.com	75	150 / 2990	10	25	20	no	yes
Heartland Payment Systems	http://www.visa-mc.com	95	0 / 249	75	22.5	15	No	A
ITransact.com	http://www.itransact.com	95	0 / 0	10	0	0	no	yes
Merchant Solutions	http://www.merchant-solution.com	75	0 / 0	10	20	15	no	yes
Merchant Capital, Inc	http://www.capital-merchant.com	0	0 / 0	9	0	10	no	A,S
MerchantChecks.com	http://merchantchecks.com	25	0 / 0	10	0	25	no	yes
Merchant Service	http://www.merchantservice.com	0	20 / 20	0	0	10	no	A,C
Northern Merchant Services	http://www.northernmerchant.com	75	159 / 159	5	125	10	no	A,S
OneCore Merchant Services	http://www.onecore.com	150	0 / 0	5	15	10	no	C
Online Credit Corp	http://www.onlinecreditcorp.com	0	0 / 0	0	0	30	yes	yes
QuickCommerce	http://www.netbiz.net	0	0 / 0	10	25	0	yes	yes
Signature Card Services	http://www.signaturecard.com	45	0 / 0	10	25	25	yes	yes
Stuart Consulting Group, Inc	http://www.stuartconsulting.com	0	0 / 0	10	15	10	no	yes
Summit Payment Solutions, LLC	http://www.summitpayment.com	15	0 / 0	0	0	0	no	yes
Technocheck Systems	http://www.technocheck.com	0	0 / 0	10	0	10	No	Yes
TransMark Corporation	http://www.transmark.com	0	0 / 0	6	15	15	no	yes
USA BankCards	http://www.usabankcards.com	0	25 / 200	8.25	20	15	Yes	Yes
Web Merchant Services	http://www.webmerchantservices.com	0	0 / 199	15	0	0	no	S,P

(*) statement/gateway fee

APP =	Application Fee	RTS	
HW / SW =	Stated Hardware / Software Cost	A =	AuthorizeNet
MSF =	Monthly Statement Fee	C =	CyberCash
MM =	Monthly Minimum Processing Fee	I =	iTransact
CBF =	Chargeback Fee	L =	LinkPoint
INTL =	Works with International Merchants	M =	MerchantLink
RTS =	Real-Time Service Compatibility	P =	Plug n Pay
		S =	Signio / Verisign (same company)

208

Chapter 15

Some people I've talked to were under the impression they'd have online real-time credit card processing capabilities as part of their merchant account—but in most cases, these are two separate (but related) things. Usually you will get your merchant account with the bank and sign up with a separate company to enable online credit card processing.

* * * WARNING * * *
Merchant accounts are not "compatible" with all processing services!

If you're going to implement online credit card processing, I recommend you find out which processing service you want to use first, then make sure to get a merchant account which is compatible with that service.

Often the processing service company will have a list of compatible merchant account providers, or sometimes they'll just tell you, "make sure the merchant account is compatible with the "Nova (or whatever) network."

Here are a few of the better-known credit card processing services:

AuthorizeNet: http://www.authorizenet.com

VeriSign: http://www.verisign.com

CyberCash: http://www.cybercash.com

SecureTrans: http://www.securetrans.com

Ibill: http://www.ibill.com

No-merchant-account-required services

There are services available which allow your customers to use a credit card to purchase your products/services without you having a merchant account. The general idea is to enter into a "resale" agreement with one of these companies. So anytime someone clicks on the "buy now" button on your website, they are technically purchasing the product from your "resale" partner and not from you directly.

The service forwards the money to you less their "commission" (usually between 5% and 15% of the sale amount). There are four main disadvantages to this system:

1) Less flexibility in the ordering system. You are forced to use whatever order system they supply.

2) Your name does not appear on the cardholder's statement—the service company's name does. Your customer may get confused and, believing it to be a fraudulent charge, initiate a chargeback.

3) It takes longer for you to get your money. With your own merchant account, you get the funds within 2-3 days of processing the charge. With these services, it may be 2-4 weeks or longer.

4) On a per-sale basis, it costs you more. The higher your volume, the more expensive this option is when compared to having your own merchant account.

> **note**: If you are just getting started and don't want to go through the expense and paperwork of obtaining your own merchant account, these No-Merchant-Account-Required services can be an attractive alternative.

Even though there are some disadvantages, there are cases where it's a good way to go. If for some reason you just can't get your own merchant account, then this option is certainly better than not taking credit cards at all.

I actually started out by using "MultiCards." Sometimes it was painful waiting for my money, but the service worked out well for me.

Chapter 15

Here are some of the better ones:

http://www.ccnow.com [Non-U.S. too.]

http://eumerchants.com [Non-U.S. too.]

http://www.multicards.com

http://www.merchantbiz.com

http://www.ibill.com

http://www.digibuy.com (includes digital product delivery!)

http://www.regsoft.com (for software/downloadables only)

http://nstarsolutions.com/index.htm

http://www.paypal.com (business account)

Alternative payment methods

There are a few "alternative" payment methods which are gaining popularity on the Internet. Though I doubt any of these will be used by more than a small percentage of your customers, they are worth mentioning.

PayPal: http://www.paypal.com

EmailMoney: http://www.emoneymail.com/

Tradenable: http://www.iescrow.com/

Of these three, PayPal is by far the most well-known service. In recent months they've added some very impressive features to their "business account" service, including the ability for your customers to pay you via the PayPal service with their credit card, international payments, and batch payments. These last two features may be especially interesting to people running affiliate programs, as it gives you an easy way to pay your international affiliates.

Electronic checks

Several of the real-time credit card processing services also have electronic check capabilities. If you were set-up with this option, the customer could opt to enter their check information (routing number, account number, check number, etc.) for payment directly from their checking account.

An alternative would be to have the customer send this information to you via a web form, email or fax and then create a check with one of the following electronic check programs:

ICPP: http://www.icpp.com

Checker: http://www.checkersoftware.com/

Common sense credit card fraud prevention

While some of the online payment processing companies run sophisticated fraud-prevention algorithms on all orders, they don't catch everything. If you sell software, ebooks, or anything else the customer downloads immediately after submitting their order, you're more at risk than someone selling products which are physically delivered to the customer.

Usually it works like this: the "customer" will use a stolen credit card to purchase your downloadable product. They get their "download code" or "password" immediately after the order.

A month later, your bank initiates a chargeback for that order. Upon investigation you learn the card holder didn't recognize the charge and has

Chapter 15

> **note** If you don't have too much volume, you might consider not automating the product download process. This way you can check the validity of the order before sending the product.

never heard of you or your company. Someone apparently used his or her credit card without his or her authorization. When you look up the order, you will find the thief used a "free" (and usually anonymous) email account.

Now you're out the cost of the product plus a $15-$35 chargeback fee in addition to the transaction fees. Ouch! Time to implement some fraud countermeasures.

If your volume requires you to use automated product delivery, then so be it. While you'll rarely get your money back when you do detect fraud, at least you can avoid chargebacks against your merchant account by reversing the charge on the stolen credit card.

Here are a couple things I've started doing to reduce fraudulent credit card usage:

- Require a phone number with the order for "verification purposes" and call the customer. If they're a genuine customer, they'll usually be delighted to know you take credit card fraud seriously. On the other hand, if they're trying to rip you off, they'll usually enter a bogus phone number hoping you won't actually call. When you call, you'll either get a "this number is not in service" message or you'll get someone that has never heard of the "customer" before.

- Make sure your order processing software captures the customer's IP address and includes it in the order details it sends you. When you get an order, run a trace route command on that IP address.

To do this on a Windows system, go to "Start/Programs/MS-DOS Prompt". When the MS-DOS window opens up, type "tracert 111.222.333.444" where

213

"111.222.333.444" is the IP address. Usually when you do this the system will tell you which domain name (such as abc123.com) corresponds with that IP address.

Go to the web site for that domain (http://www.abc123.com) and see if it's in the same country as your customer. Just the other day I had someone submit an order with a Kansas City, Missouri address, but they were submitting their order from an Internet Service Provider in France! Actually, that was an easy one to catch, They were using a yahoo.fr (Yahoo France) email address.

These are very simple techniques, but I've had very few problems with fraudulent orders since I started using them.

Promotional items, premiums, and incentives

16

Promotional items, premiums, and incentives

Have you ever seen one of those car dealership advertisements offering a "free 3-day/2-night Bahamas vacation with every test drive?" How are they able to pay for all those free vacations and still make money on the cars they sell? I know, I know, you're thinking something about those slick car salespeople and what the car really costs them in the first place. Bad example on my part, I suppose, but seriously, how can companies afford free vacations for people who don't even buy their product?

The answer is: "They don't pay very much for the vacation packages." If five people test drive a car, and only one buys, the dealer pays for the 5 vacation packages and still makes a profit. I'd love to tell you exactly how little these vacation packages cost, but for legal reasons I can't.

However, I have listed a few companies in the references/resources section that sell these packages. Because some of them have other distributors that sell these same packages at different prices, I can't publish their prices here—just contact them directly and find out for yourself. You'll be amazed!

Besides travel packages, there are many other "promotional items" you can give away to spice up your offers. One of the best (and lowest cost) items you can offer is an "information product" related to your product or service. These can have very high "perceived value" and can be created for next to nothing (see the section on eBook software).

Depending upon your what your main product or service is, you may be able to offer on-phone consulting time as a bonus when people make a purchase, or perhaps a newsletter subscription.

Contact the following companies about their travel incentive packages. They may have other incentive packages as well, such as savings coupon books, so be sure to ask.

Adler Travel:	http://www.freetravel.com
Fennell Promotions, Inc.:	http://www.fennellpromotions.com
Crown Marketing Group, Inc.:	http://www.crownmarketing.com/
Premium Exchange, Inc.:	http://www.premex.com/
DJC Enterprises:	http://www.djcenterprises.com

If you are interested in more traditional promotional items with your company information imprinted on them at your request, check out the following "Yahoo" category of over 200 suppliers:

http://dir.yahoo.com/Business_and_Economy/Business_to_Business/
Marketing_and_Advertising/Advertising/Promotional_Items/

Here is a small sampling of the different items you can get from these companies:

pencils	calendars	clocks	foreign coins
pens	cigarette lighters	flags	medals

Chapter 16

caps	banners	balloons	plaques
mugs	signs	banners	certificates
t-shirts	license plates	matchbooks	stamps
fine china	mouse pads	golf clubs	letter openers
sunglasses	dust covers	towels	sweats
coasters	plastic shelves	decals	tote bags
pitchers	watches	buttons	aprons
playing cards	radios	magnets	tins

Research and strategic intelligence 17

Research and strategic intelligence

Since the the Internet as we know it traces its roots to a project funded by ARPA (Advanced Research Projects Agency), it's no surprise the Internet is such a powerful research tool today. The Internet (and specifically the "World Wide Web") is growing at an astounding rate, with over 1 billion web pages available at the time of publication.

You can do research on just about any topic of course, but in this guide I focus on business-related research such as marketing and trends, customer feedback, consumer research, and business intelligence. Strategic intelligence could be a section of its own, but because of its heavy dependence on research, I've decided to include it here.

How do you sift through the mountains of data to find that one golden nugget of information? Use the right tools of course. In this chapter I will be sharing a number of online resources, software tools, and services for efficient and effective research and strategic intelligence. First, we'll discuss research in general, then strategic intelligence specifically.

General research

I want to start out with an article from Cheryl Jack. I've never met Cheryl, but at one time she was a frequent contributor to a business discussion board I visited, and she always had such great resources to share with us. I often found myself saying, "Where does she get all this stuff?"

Naturally, she was the first person I thought of to ask for an article on this subject—thankfully, she obliged.

While this article could actually be a whole chapter on research (that's what I originally asked Cheryl to do), I expanded the scope of this chapter a bit—so look for some more information on the topic after Cheryl's article.

How to Effectively Research Any Topic

By Cheryl Jack

SeriousAboutSuccess.com

Designing any successful product or service requires time well spent in research. This not only helps to appropriately target your markets, it allows you to uncover the hot buttons of your prospect. It also keeps you from wasting time on products or services that just drain your resources.

> **note** Research is a broad word. It covers not only the academic facts behind the idea, but it can also include experience (interactivity)—not only that gained by yourself, but also of others too.

The question that was posed to me was, "How do you do research?" Actually, the more appropriate question is, "What is your system for doing research?" A system can be taught and duplicated by anyone. However there is one thing that I cannot teach you, and it entails:

Curiosity

To do effective research, you must have a natural curiosity to want to know the reasons why and the reasons *who*, *what*, *when*, *where*, and *how*. It's like mining for gold. You always start with a premise, a direction, and you must

Chapter 17

never be afraid of changing your direction, your hypothesis, and your goals if your research indicates otherwise. Making course corrections is just plain wise. Pilots do it. So do major corporations. One important difference is that you and I have the luxury of being able to make course corrections faster than major corporations—and bail out of bad ideas sooner.

Well, before we get well on our way to the meat of this section, you might be asking yourself right now, "Who are you to tell me this? What makes you qualified?" Good question. I'll elaborate a bit.

I guess you can say that I am no fly-by-night researcher. I have loads of experience in the field including having done formal scientific research, including a project funded by the March of Dimes (a study of the teratogenicity of a food additive). I've done research in the field of medicine, psychiatry and ethics. I also have done loads of research in sports performance and bodybuilding, and privately trained others. I research communities, locales, peoples, lifestyles, and a whole bunch of other interests. I live a life of a researcher, which I find somewhat akin to an explorer. To me, it's a lot of fun and hard work—and I'm not averse to hard work. The rewards are great. The freedom, wonderful. The diversity is constantly stimulating. It is like living a dream lifestyle, one of change and challenge. This is the way I choose my life to be. It doesn't have to be exactly this way for you because you define your dreams.

The purpose of this article is to show you a blueprint, of sorts, of how to do research. I will start at the beginning and pepper our journey with resources that you will want to use. Once you know the process, applying yourself to it will reap rewards. However, I want to issue one caution: Never take anyone's word for anything.

I'm sure that you've seen many a website that have a list of links with no explanation about why you should visit them. And when you click on the links listed, you find that the site is down or worse—it's just horrendous. Obviously, the humans that actually recommended those sites never visited them before. If they did, they wouldn't have recommended them, right?

You have also heard experts giving diametrically opposing *opinions* regarding a myriad of topics. We still call them *experts*? Get used to using your own brain to analyze all the data you collect, and make your own deductions. Make sure what you use makes sense. Throw away preconceived notions, but start with a good premise.

Well, let's get started with the first section on how to do research. Understand that we will be limiting our discussion mainly to market research on Internet-based products.

Section One: How to do Research

Before you begin your quest, decide what it is that you are looking to accomplish, and decide what medium you want to display it in. Why this additional step? If it is a more visual medium, you may want to make note of graphs, charts, and pictures versus just raw data. You also want to check permissions, whether you need to ask who ever developed that visual aid for permission to reproduce it. It is annoying to try to remember where you found something after you have pages and pages of support material in a file.

> *note* Try to be narrow rather than broad. Know your audience, and tailor your research for them.

If you are interested in compiling information about, let's say, bungee jumping, decide what you want to cover in light of who is your target audience. If I was designing a product for avid bungee jumpers, I do not need to cover any of the basics. However, a beginner just might want to know a little more about the mechanics, the cord, and the insurance coverage issue. An avid bungee jumper just might want to know about the top 10 places in the world to bungee, and what makes them so awesome.

Now, before we go too far, let's talk about what you will need to really do good research.

Chapter 17

Back before the web, I did almost all of my research in graduate school libraries due to the sheer availability of resources, resource people and a research librarian. Nowadays, I usually start on the net and then go offline. So, a good library and a good research librarian are priceless. You can find periodicals, journals, books and magazines there. A librarian can do a search for the topic you are interested in, and many can search back to the early 60's for articles. They can even order books/periodicals they do not have and are usually quite happy to help out.

Having a reliable computer and backup device are also paramount. Since what can happen usually does, plan on thwarting unexpected computer problems by utilizing the boy scout's first rule and *be prepared*. Have a reliable backup device, and use it frequently.

Always make sure that you make several copies of your data, and keep one copy at a different location than where your computer lives. I cannot tell you all the tragic losses I've experienced by not paying serious attention to this rule consistently and how much time and money it has cost me to find a solution. Sometime, there isn't any solution, just lost effort. One marketer I know lost his entire mailing list to an office fire. Yes, he had backed up his data. Unfortunately, his back-up disk was in the office that burned.

I've personally experienced early computer death by freaky occurrences (hard drive failures, hard drives folding in on themselves, lightning, and the still unexplained booting failure). I guarantee that when you can least afford it is when something like this will happen.

It's Murphy's Law in action. Ever since living through the last one of these freak-out times (my book was in the computer that crashed), I've adopted a more defensive posture. Subsequently, less of this type of surprise happens.

> *note* — Back-up your data and your bookmark files, and remember to make full use of your history file.

I cannot urge you enough to utilize this easy feature of your web browsers. Take a look at where your history file lives in Netscape and Internet

227

Explorer. There will be a box that states how many days to keep your links in history. The default setting is usually ridiculously low, like 8. I usually put this to 600. This means that the browser will automatically track and make a record of where I go for nearly 2 years before starting to purge links. Since I usually finish a project way before this amount of time has lapsed, I can happily explore every whim I have without a care. If I remember what day or week I found an interesting resource, but somehow forgot to note it elsewhere, I just peruse my history file. It has saved the day many a time. I also clean my history file because I visit certain sites over and over again. There is no need for me to have 300 repetitive links to Gorp.org—I will remember them.

> **note** The time to get your computer serviced or to have a memory upgrade is before you begin this type of project.

I've heard of people losing data in an upgrade. My computer guys usually backup my hard drive before doing this. However, not all do. You can usually add peripherals without a problem.

Keep a pad of paper (preferably the type you flip up) by your computer and where you do your offline research. Keep another one in your car and one at your daytime job. You never know when an aberrant thought, a fleeting idea or a phenomenal resource will turn up. Too many of us are used to just using the bookmark function of our web browsers or highlighting a book/magazine (make sure that it belongs to you). Neither of these methods is good enough.

And there is just something about putting thoughts on paper that helps to make them real, gives them form and substance, and just seems to allow your mind to use them as a scaffold for further exploration. It has worked wonders for my current project, which started simply as an audiotape. Today, I have seven other

> **HINT** Keep a pad close by for recording these important resources. This way, you can easily find the high points and other things you might want to give further thought to.

projects launching around this theme, just because I paid attention to the spurious thoughts I had while developing it.

We each have a time of day that we are most optimized, like a well-groomed thoroughbred. This time of day is what I'll refer to as *peak performance time*. Are you a morning person, an evening person or an early morning person? Is there more than one time of the day that you are razor sharp and the most efficient?

> **note** By noticing when you get the most done, you can fine tune your working pattern. Doing research during these times will be the most productive use of energy and it will shorten development time of your project.

Be very jealous of your workspace. I do not allow anyone to come into my workspace. Being on the road constantly, I wage the war I call the battle of the maids. Others have spouses that believe neatness is the way to spiritual enlightenment or nirvana. In other households, little monsters . . . er . . . should I say "kids" rule, getting into everything. Your workspace is like a canvas. You are creating a masterpiece there. It is not subject to the regular rules of engagement as the other spaces in your home.

> **E-Z TIP** Make sure that anyone else living in your household helps support you in your work by respecting the sanctity of your workspace.

Finally, manage the phone. When I am doing research, usually for a product or a presentation, I disconnect the phone line that rings. In the past, I have turned off the ringer and set it to a silent answering machine. When I am on call at the hospital, I let them know that I plan to be on the computer that night and instruct them to page me first. This works really well as it allows me to finish sifting through an idea and make a record of it before I use my second line to call in.

We have set the stage for the workspace and how to maximize your efforts. Let's now get to a blueprint for doing research, both on and offline.

Section two: Nuggets and gems— where to find them

You are sitting by your computer with an idea, trying to figure out where you should go to find out more about your target audience, your market and how you can grow it. You are pretty sure that the niche is a good one, but you are not so sure that you are on the right track. What should you do?

Obviously, you will want to collect information. You need historical information to get the basis of whatever you are looking for. Then you need to get timely information as to what is going on in that field today. You will to peek into the minds of your prospective customers to identify their wants. And finally, you want information that peers into the future, so you can figure out where that market will be and what it will be demanding.

When I have an idea in a niche that I think is hot, I want to immerse myself in everything I can find about it and better focus my idea. So, what I end up doing is identifying where I can get a constant stream of targeted information about whatever niche interests me. This way, I have a much higher chance of launching a successful product idea. Where do I go?

Here are several choices:

1) **Search Engines:** I put this first because that is usually where you will find most of what follows. Search engines are like the card catalogues of the Internet. There are literally hundreds of them out there with more starting all the time. Keeping them relevant is a major undertaking. Here are a few that I choose to use.

I still like Dogpile.com as the best overall engine for doing research. It is a multiengine search engine. It is like a one-stop-shop for information. I know that a lot is said about the *Open Directory* (dmoz.org) operated

Chapter 17

by Netscape, but I haven't been impressed one bit. I also still find a lot of information at NorthernLight.com, including a lot of very technical data. This is where I found Venhuzen's treatise on sand filtration septic systems and his personal contact information. Be aware that there can be a lot of outdated and irrelevant pages here. It seems like a lot of their good content is premium content.

If I just want to find one thing, like a web address or software manufacturer's site, and I'm not sure I have all my data right, then I will go for a direct hit at either Google.com, DirectHit.com, or GoTo.com. If I am just looking for a merchant for a particular type of merchandise, then GoTo is where I go. Be prepared to really put in some time here. You really want to master the right click (always open another browser window from the link results page).

> **note** — Make sure that your computer has enough memory to not crash with 15 browser windows open.

Another search engine to test drive is AllTheWeb.com as it can come up with some very targeted replies. Galaxy.com claims to come up with only relevant searches. I tested it and there was a paucity of real data in this one. However, what it did come up with was something I hadn't seen before.

One other site that I have just been amazed at for the amount of stuff available is www.InfoJump.com. I am spending more time here just because there is so much here to check out. InfoJump is a search engine for magazine and newspaper articles and will also search message boards and ezines for articles of interest. Right now, they claim a database of 5 million articles and 4,000 publications.

231

Remember all the pay-per-click search engines? You can expect the relevancy to be higher than regular search engines because people pay to be listed in the appropriate categories. GoTo is the most successful example of this type of search engine. GoTo has a page that can suggest alternative key words and rate their relevancy. I use it to test other key words and to find information from vendors who are using those words. Then just make a list of the keyword gems and use them to do research in the other search engines.

Make sure to check out the other pay-per-click search engines like FindWhat.com, Bay9.com, Kanoodle.com, and Ah-ha.com. No one engine is best for everything. Experiment.

2) **Discussion Lists:** 2 types: newsletter version and newsgroup version (see below).

You also learn what really concerns these people, just in case they are not your target audience. A product has a better chance of being a successful one if they are your target audience. This way, you already know what concerns people who would want your product. And, you know how to talk to them in their own language. You can better design a product with a passion that your audience can identify with.

Another good thing about discussion lists is instant feedback. When I had a problem with my digital piano, I went to a Roland newsgroup and posted a question. I had several interesting answers in a couple of days, including a suggestion for a new synthesizer. They also told me what the problems were of users of the suggested synthesizer. So, if I were going to design a product, I already knew what they wanted to buy right now.

As for discussion lists, they've all been either too chatty or too boring for me. I've unsubscribed to all except one. The reason I stay is because of the quality of persons I tend to meet there. The list is for networking and doing business. You might want to join and see if FrankelBiz (www.frankelbiz.com) is for you.

Chapter 17

You can always unsubscribe to newsletters and discussion lists if they do not suit you. Plus, many discussion lists are too chatty or just ask the same thing over and over. So, you either tire of them or outgrow them.

3) **Electronic newsletters:** What you will find out by getting ezines (electronic newsletters) and participating in discussion lists is what those people are talking about and whether or not this is where your target audience hangs out. Yes, they may share a common interest. However, those people may never pay for anything that costs over two cents. You know what I mean. This may be an audience, but not your audience.

Now, one of the problems with electronic newsletters is that you cannot always find one that specifically targets your niche. There won't be one listed in any ezine directory you've tracked down. What do you do? This is when hanging out in newsgroups will help. Many of those regulars know where others of similar interest meet and if there are any ezine lists. They can also point you to websites of interest and discussion boards you may never find anywhere else. So, make sure that you always use proper etiquette in the newsgroups.

Over the past four years, I've gone through a lot of newsletters. There are so many that I've been quite liberal and forgiving with, expecting greatness but only getting a "ho hum." Some of these got nuked. Others got saved for the day I could scan them for a morsel or two. Most I lost interest in, if I ever did have interest in them at all. A few remain as keepers for a variety of different reasons. Many times your nuggets (data) will come from a less targeted source.

Here are a few newsletters that may interest you:

TrendWatch: www.trendwatch.com – the name says it all.

RedHerring: www.redherring.com – this is totally about ebusiness and what the movers are doing. Pay attention to who is acquiring what will give you clues as to where the market is moving.

233

The Standard: www.thestandard.com - the bible for keeping up with everything that is happening in the electronic universe. Make sure you subscribe to the print version.

A Marketing Idea A Day: www.ideasiteforbusiness.com - this newsletter not only gives you marketing ideas but can show you new vendors and many new ideas.

Jesse Berst's Anchor Desk: www.zdnet.com - fresh and fun. It is a way to keep up on what is important in the net universe.

ResearchBuzz: www.researchbuzz.com - I keep this one to see where their mind is going. Sometimes, I am clued into a real treasure. You just never know what is going to turn up here.

Online Community Report: www.onlinecommunityreport.com - this is a must for anyone building or planning to build a content site. However, it is also of interest to see who is developing what and what direction some of the larger communities or membership sites are going in. It is also a way to track trends.

eMarketer: www.eMarketer.com - a really good newsletter about marketing on the net and what the movers and shakers are doing.

Database Central Gazette: www.searchdatabase.com - another tool for catching weird and trendy things.

dBusiness: www.dBusiness.com - I use this to track the pulse of a community. Right now, there are several incubators in Austin and Denver that I track. These guys come out with some timely products. I want to know about them before most others do.

CNet: Take your pick at www.cnet.com - e-commerce news giant. You can get more news than you can keep up with from Cnet. And now that you can target what you get, you can cut out all the stuff you don't.

Analogx: analogx.com - they design tools that help me as a webmaster. Their tools can be used to do research on potential competitors or collaborators.

Boogie Jack: boogiejack.com - this guy can do some good graphic work although his recent change in his website doesn't reflect it. Lots of down home humor and some graphic design tips. He occasionally can give you a real marketing gem.

Big Nose Bird: bignosebird.com - I've been with them and touted their praises long before they became a part of Really Big. Primarily for scripting and graphic design, it also can have a marketing pearl and just some overall comments. I always read this one when it comes.

Publish: publish.com - discusses online and offline publishing and previews new technology in this field.

Business Thinkers: businessthinkers.com - fairly new ezine. Can offer interesting freebies like teleseminars with PR gurus like Raleigh Pinsky. I'm not sure in what direction they are going. However, I like that I cannot predict that. I've met some very interesting people through this newsletter and expanded my knowledge base.

4) **Targeted Response Bots:** These are my most favorite ways of keeping track with what is happening in the niches I am interested in, next to newsfeeds. (See next section.)

What is a targeted response bot? Actually, these are robots or spider programs that you can tell to go out on the net and fetch the information you are looking for, well, automatically. Most will send you a daily dose of information that matches your key words.

These response bots are time savers. I tend to look at them first before perusing the more general newsletters I have. Some of these robots are better than others. Usually fine tuning them a bit (adjusting your key

235

words) results in a higher amount of good resources. I prefer those that will continue to send me information on a daily basis until I tell them to stop. You will have to try your hands to see what works for you.

My current favorites are: Tracerlock (www.peacefire.org) and CNet Alerts (new but awesome in certain categories). It is amazing as to the variety of information they send. Both are free services.

Another great service I've been trying out recently is eTours.com. They send you a continuous flow of good websites of interest in your area of interest. There is a lot that this site potentially offers.

Here are a few of what is out there:

Northern Lights alerts: testing currently; only sends info when it has something noteworthy. Therefore do not expect daily messages. I use this for my 'heavier' topics.

eLibrary Tracker: sporadic; not impressed with results.

dBusiness: lots of info on the market sector of interest.

TVeyes: results will time out; you have to constantly return to the website to recharge your option; this is annoying.

5) **Newsfeeds:** These are different than electronic newsletters. Newsfeeds come in two general flavors: subscription or web based. The subscription version will send you your information daily or twice daily on your topic(s) of interest. Most allow tighter customization of your topics. You will get headlines targeted for your niche fed directly to a web page on your site or to you via email (www.Moreover.com).

> **note** The trend is towards paid newsfeeds. I see more of these popping up.

Chapter 17

One service requires that you become a member to check your newsfeed online (www.Excite.com).

And yet others offer tickers for your site. Newsfeeds are one of the best research tools available. The downside: only so much data is archived. So it is better for topics that are hot or trendy, i.e., in the news, over the past 6-9 months.

6) **Research Reports:** These can be pricey but there are several services that also offer a free version (usually requires that you sign up to gain access to that portion of their website) and newsletters. I currently get the IT Forecaster from IDC.com and the newsletter by Forrester Research (Forrester.com). Gomez Advisors recently changed their website (Gomez.com) to more commercial versus more research oriented. I'm not sure what they are doing with their reports section as I could not find it.

Again, more of these research firms are popping up on the net. And most are charging around $1000 per report. They are gearing their content to the corporate markets.

7) **Discussion Forums:** They are around and are helpful in finding out if you are on track with your idea. I use them to stay in touch with the concerns of my audience, although I am spending much less time in these nowadays. Some of these are worthy of your subscription and some have digest versions.

Many discussion forums are not listed in any forum database. You will find out about them through casual online chats with persons who share your interest. Many times you will find these people at other forums. This is one reason that signature files and links attached to posts can be absolute gold mines of information.

There is one up and coming discussion forum where lots of very bright persons hang out, including expert copywriters and product developers. Make sure you visit the Seeds of Wisdom discussion forum at SowPub.com.

237

8) **Magazines:** Yes, the offline world still exists. I find that many of the print magazines that have ezines do not put their best content out for free massive consumption. In fact, certain magazines come out so frequently that keeping up is really a task. One of my favorite to peruse is *The Standard* (warning: do not subscribe to the print version unless you are willing to receive volumes of data; the publishing schedule is weekly). I also peruse *Red Herring, Yahoo Internet Life, Wired* (has improved over the past year), *Business Week, Publish,* and *Computer VideoMaker*. It is amazing what little tidbits of information you can find on a variety of subject matters in these magazines. You also want to pay attention to the advertisements in many of these publications, especially for research.

I recently subscribed to eCompany and have been very pleased with them. I find that they profile ebusinesses—successful, unsuccessful and hopeful. I use it to spot trends, as I do with *Red Herring* and *The Standard*. My favorite print geek magazine is *Maximum PC*. I will not buy a peripheral or upgrade until I know what these guys say. I've been a follower since *Boot*, even though games are not my thing. Their candid and opinionated format is refreshing.

Business 2.0 was recently launched and is interesting. It assumes that you are not a newbie. You might want to follow it for the ideas it can give you. *Time* also has a net themed magazine which I browse rather than read.

Also note that there are many magazines that are being given away to attract those interested in those specific niches. And some of these magazines are not lightweights. You might be surprised to find magazines like *eWeek, Inter@ctive Week, Software Development,* and *Audio/Video Magazine* are all freebies. If you are into CAD, there are several free magazines for this field. And I just got a solicitation for a magazine for CTO (chief technical officers).

9) **Books:** Topic/niche specific. Use Amazon.com and BarnesandNoble.com to research what is happening in your field, who has the latest book out, and to easily research what has been written.

Your librarian can perform a more extensive search of what has been published over the past two decades. But the online booksellers will show you what is hot now.

R.R.Bowker (www.bowker.com) is also online. You can look up publishers, find out what is scheduled to come out in print form and what is out-of-print. There really isn't a better resource of this kind. You can order the books-in-print CD from their site as well as several of their other databases. You'll find them at Bowker.com.

Regarding print newsletter databases—an online database is at AccessNewsletters.com. A hardcopy directory is available. Ask for the Oxbridge Directory of Newsletters.

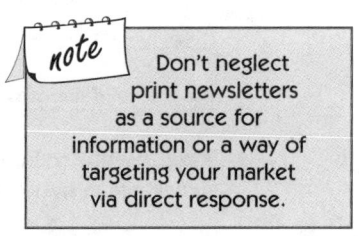

> **note** Don't neglect print newsletters as a source for information or a way of targeting your market via direct response.

10) **Workshops/Seminars/Trade shows:** Topic/niche specific. This is one of the very best ways I know of getting info that most people in your niche just do not have. Plus I can ask specific questions pertinent to whatever I am working on. It is a way of having an expert collaborate with you on your next project. Not only have I learned cutting edge stuff from the best in the world, I got to network with a whole bunch of other folks who have contacts that I would not have been introduced to any other way. It has spawned ideas for collaborations and joint ventures.

11) **Expert Sites:** Yes, the "guru" sites are springing up all over the net. These usually work by you posting a question and one of the experts will answer it online. You can peruse the archives on several of these sites, which is another way of doing research. And in one way, it is even better than answering your own questions, as you will know what others are asking and what the average knowledge base of your prospects are, as well as what their burning desires are. Here are a few "ask me" expert sites that just might be of interest to you:

www.AskMe.com

www.Experts.com

www.Guru.com

www.ExpertsCentral.com

www.Exp.com

Aska Locator (www.Vrd.org/locator)

www.KnowPost.com

www.About.com – formerly The Mining Company site. If you are not sure where to start doing research, head here. It will give you ideas.

www.Surf-Guru.com

Section three: Tools of the trade

Doing research from your desktop can be a hassle if organization isn't your forte. And when ideas are springing forth, especially if you are like a bloodhound on a trail, well, organization can suffer for enthusiasm. Lucky for us, there are several tools that help to make the process easier.

We discussed using the search engines as tools for doing research. This can be further optimized in several ways. One is to bring a searching utility to your desktop. There are several you may want to look at. Bulls Eye (www.intelliseek.com) is a desktop version of their search engine. Copernic (www.copernic.com)is another highly touted desktop utility search engine utility. Zeus (www.cyber-Robotics.com) is a robot program that you can train to gather links and makes a link directory.

I tend to use Dogpile.com for most things. However, I've become quite partial to 2bpop (www.2bpop.com). This is the only program I know of that eliminates duplicate links before it brings you the results. You can either click those results right away, or put them into your SpotOn (www.spoton.com) enabled browser for faster viewing. If I am doing an extended research, then I will want to know who has linked to each of those sites. This is where Web Ferret Pro (www.ferretsoft.com) excels. I put my results from 2bPop into it to generate an extended list of who is linking to the sites I am interested in and explore their contents.

Now that I have all sorts of information gathered, I can either snake a copy of the information with an application like Web Snake (www.anawave.com), use the built-in webpage copy utility in IE 5 or Netscape 4.7, or go one step better to eGems. eGems (www.egems.com) is the best program I have seen that allows me to organize all the data I gather from the web. It not only can copy link locations, but it also can recall from where data was cited. eGems can copy images and text into an organized file for your projects. All info can be easily arranged in it and dragged and dropped into documents at will. It is a revolutionary piece of software for organizing research done via the net. It can even capture/transfer info from email. I bought it right after reviewing the flash demo, without even trying it. It's that good.

Flyswat (www.flyswat.com) is a new tool that will turn words on your screen (email and browsers) into links. These links will allow you to get more information about the item. Right now it seems as though it will have more of a commercial application than a research application, but who knows what it will become in the near future.

Closing comments

Now that you have completed this phase of your research, you will need to format that information for your audience. Make it easy for them to access it. Most word processing formats can be converted to PDF (Adobe portable document format). And HTML (hypertext markup language) can be converted to PDF too. If you are going to print it, test the font and make sure the wording is clear. Read it out loud and correct anything that doesn't flow right. And as always, start collecting data for the revision after you publish this version.

Good luck in all your research endeavors.

Cheryl Jack

©2000 SeriousAboutSuccess.com

Besides those listed in the above article, here are a couple more services that notify you when changes are made to the web sites you specify:

http://www.clippingservice.com

http://www.c-4-u.com

The below services will send you a regular report of new online content related to topics or keywords you specify. The results come from online newspapers, magazines, ezines, newswires, search engines, and web sites.

http://www.clippingservice.com

http://www.webclipping.com

http://www.cyberalert.com

http://www.spyonit.com/Home

http://www.cyberclipping.com

Search engines/directories

Though it may seem obvious, no discussion of online research would be complete without at least mentioning the online search engines and directories. With "directories," each site has been evaluated by a real live person before being included in the directory. Because "search engines" add sites without human evaluation, they have many more sites, but the relevance of each site to the topic you're searching may not be as good.

Chapter 17

The first three sites listed below are directories, the rest are search engines:

http://www.yahoo.com

http://www.about.com

http://www.looksmart.com

http://www.google.com

http://www.infoseek.com

http://www.northernlight.com

http://www.hotbot.com

http://www.altavista.com

http://www.snap.com

http://www.alltheweb.com

Meta search sites—these sites will query several sites for your search term and return the results of all of them—are a great time saver.

http://www.dogpile.com

http://www.infind.com

http://www.ixquick.com

http://www.gogettem.com (formerly super-seek.com)

http://www.metacrawler.com

http://www.savvysearch.com

http://www.allinonesearch.com

To see a comparison of the various directory and search engines (many more than I've included here), visit Michael Campbell's site:

http://searchenginepositioning.com

This site was designed for those interested in search engine positioning (covered in the next section), but it offers a wealth of information regarding search engine popularity which may be useful in this discussion as well.

Last but not least, don't forget about the Copernic, 2bpop, and WebFerret Software mentioned in Cheryl's article—they are very powerful tools for searching online.

Strategic intelligence

When I first started this section, I had intended to discuss "competitive intelligence." In my research I discovered intelligence of a much broader scope is required. In his book *Millennium Intelligence*, Jerry Miller defines the aspects of intelligence:

Strategic intelligence emphasizes its relationship to strategic decision making and business and/or product development.

Business intelligence incorporates the monitoring of a wide range of developments across an organization's external business environment or marketplace.

Competitive intelligence focuses on the present and potential strengths, weaknesses and activities of organizations with similar products or services within a single industry.

Competitor intelligence involves profiling a specific organization.

Chapter 17

Now a disclaimer—several books have been written about this topic, and it's beyond the scope of this guide to cover it in detail. The resources I provide here are excellent, but they won't tell you how to prepare for or implement effective intelligence gathering. I'd strongly recommend you get Jerry's book (or other books on the same topic—however, Jerry's is the best I've seen thus far).

Here are several resources to aid you in conducting your own strategic intelligence operations online.

Quick profiles on over 900,000 public and private companies:

http://www.companiesonline.com/

The Thomas Register of American Manufacturers is a great resource for finding who makes what. Do a search by brand name or product/service name. You can also get the contact and company profile information. Registration is required, but it's free.

http://www.thomasregister.com

Insite Pro allows you unlimited access to seven business information databases for a flat fee. Unfortunately, they don't state what that fee is on their site. It may be dependent on how many researchers you have at your company.

http://www.insitepro.com

Lexis-Nexis is one of the "major" database searching sites. They have a number of pricing plans, including instant access which is $24/day to $69/day, depending on the databases you use. If you're going to be using them more than occasionally, you should look into their flat-rate service.

http://www.lexis-nexis.com

245

Dow Jones Interactive charges $69.00 per year for access to their "basic" search functions. They have additional per-transaction charges for various other reports and services. A wealth of information here.

http://www.djinteractive.com/

To get the SEC filing information of U.S. companies, go to the following site and click on the "EDGAR Database" link:

http://www.sec.gov/

CompanySleuth will monitor activity from companies you specify, and alert you when anything of interest relevant to that company is discovered in "stock quotes, news, insider trades, domain, trademarks and patent registrations and message boards." The service is free. (Hint: You could also specify your own company if you want to see what other people are saying about you.)

http://www.companysleuth.com

Want to find out how a customer's experience differs at your competitor's site from your own? Check out Vividence. They'll send target customers to your and your competitor's site. Then they'll get feedback from those customers, analyze their experiences, and tell you what you should be doing differently.

http://www.vividence.com

To monitor your competition's advertising, try these services:

http://www.digitrends.net/adalert

http://www.adrelevance.com

I'll close with an article which may or may not fit in this section, but it's closely related. This article explains how to use the search engines to find which sites link to a specified web site. This helps you to determine who's linking to your site, and it also allows you to find out who's linking to your competitor's site. Perhaps, you can get some of the same places to link to your site.

Measuring link popularity

By Sumantra Roy

"Which search engines use link popularity as a factor in ranking pages?"

Well, that question has become pretty moot these days. Just about every search engine uses link popularity as a factor. So, how do you find out how much link popularity your site has? And how do you know which sites are actually linking to you? In this article, I'll tell you how you can find out the link popularity of your site in the 11 major search engines.

1. AltaVista

In order to find out the number of sites linking to the domain mysite.com in AltaVista, you would type in link:mysite.com in AltaVista's search box. If you wish to exclude links from pages within the mysite.com domain, you would type in link:mysite.com -url:mysite.com.

If you want to find out how many sites are linking to a particular page (i.e. mypage.html) in the mysite.com domain, you would type in:

   link:mysite.com/mypage.html.

Again, in order to exclude links from pages within the mysite.com domain, you would type in

   link:mysite.com/mypage.html -url:mysite.com.

Note that you should not type in the "www" or the "http://" prefixes.

2. AOL

There is no special command to measure link popularity in AOL. You can consider typing in mysite.com to measure the links to mysite.com, but you will get highly inaccurate results.

3. Excite

There is no way you can find out the link popularity of your site in Excite. This is because Excite does not return the number of sites which match the search criterion. Furthermore, like AOL, there is no special command for measuring link popularity.

4. Google

In order to find out the number of sites linking to mysite.com in Google, you would type in link:mysite.com.

If you want to find out how many sites are linking to the page mypage.html in the mysite.com domain, you would type in link:mysite.com/mypage.html. However, there is no way you can exclude links from pages within the www.mysite.com domain from being counted.

You should not type in the "www" prefix in Google. However, including the "http://" prefix is permissible. It will not change the results.

5. HotBot

There are two methods of measuring link popularity in Hotbot. In the first case, in order to find out the number of sites linking to mysite.com, you can type in linkdomain:mysite.com. In order to exclude links from pages within the mysite.com domain, you can use:

linkdomain:mysite.com -domain:mysite.com.

Chapter 17

Make sure that you do not use the "www" or "http://" prefixes when you use this method.

However, this method cannot be used to find out the number of links to specific pages in your site (i.e., you cannot use this method to find out the links to the page mypage.html in the domain mysite.com).

In order to find out the number of links to specific pages, choose "links to this URL" from the "Look for" drop-down combo box and then type in the complete URL (i.e. http://www.mysite.com/mypage.html) in the search box. In order to exclude links from within the mysite.com domain, type http://www.mysite.com/mypage.html-domain:mysite.com in the search box after choosing "links to this URL" from the combo box. Note that for the second method, you need to use the "*http://*" prefix.

Lastly, you should note that in the second method, typing http://www.mysite.com will only find links to the home page of the www.mysite.com domain, and not any of the other pages.

6. Infoseek

The method of measuring link popularity in Infoseek is exactly the same as in AltaVista.

7. Lycos

In order to measure link popularity in Lycos, first click on the Advanced Search link below the search box. To find out the number of sites linking to mysite.com in Lycos, you would type in ml:mysite.com in the search box. If you wish to exclude links from pages within the mysite.com domain, you would type in ml:mysite.com -h:mysite.com.

If you want to find out how many sites are linking to a particular page (say, mypage.html) in the mysite.com domain, you would type in

249

ml:mysite.com/mypage.html. Again, in order to exclude links from pages within the mysite.com domain, you would type in:

> ml:mysite.com/mypage.html -h:mysite.com

Note that you should not type in the "www" or the "http://" prefixes.

8. MSN

The method of measuring link popularity in MSN is almost the same as that in Hotbot. The first method is exactly the same. For the second method, click on the "More Options" tab, type in the complete URL in the "Search the web for:" text box and choose "links to URL" from the "Find:" drop-down combo box. However, unlike Hotbot, you cannot eliminate links from pages within the same domain using the second method.

Note that the "More Options" tab is displayed only after you search for something in MSN. It is not displayed in MSN's home page.

9. Netscape

Netscape is a directory based engine. It takes its results from the Open Directory. If no results are found in the Open Directory, it takes its results from Google. Since it is a directory based engine, the concept of measuring link popularity is not all that meaningful. You can type in link:mysite.com to measure the number of links to the domain mysite.com. In this case, Netscape will simply take its results from Google.

10. Northern Light

There is no special command for measuring link popularity in Northern Light. To get a very approximate idea of the number of sites linking to the domain mysite.com, you can type in mysite.com. In order to eliminate the references to the mysite.com domain from within the domain, you can type in mysite.com -url:mysite.com.

Chapter 17

To get an approximate measure of the number of links to the page mypage.html in the domain mysite.com, you can type in: mysite.com/mypage.html in the search box. Again, to eliminate the references to the page from within the mysite.com domain, you would type mysite.com/mypage.html -url:mysite.com

Don't type in the "http://" or "www" prefixes.

11. Webcrawler

There is no way you can find out the link popularity of your site in Webcrawler. This is because, like Excite, Webcrawler does not return the number of sites which match the search criterion. Also, there is no special command for measuring link popularity.

Article by Sumantra Roy. Sumantra is a search engine positioning specialist. For free articles on search engine placement, subscribe to his 1st Search Ranking Newsletter by sending a blank email to mailto:1stSearch_Ranking-subscribe@listbot.com or by going to http://www.1stSearch_Ranking.com

251

Search engine positioning

18

18
Search engine positioning

Ask 20 internet marketing experts "How important is search engine positioning in your overall promotion strategy?" You'll likely get 20 different answers. For some, it's the only thing that matters, but for others, it's not part of their strategy at all. While I think we should work on search engine positioning, I think it should be part of a well-balanced promotional effort.

One thing everyone agrees to is that with few exceptions, the days of getting good positioning without trying are over. It was easy once, but now that the law of supply and demand has kicked in, it takes a lot more work. However, if you're willing to do the work, you can still get good enough positioning to make it worth your while.

Search engine expert Michael Campbell has graciously allowed me to include two of his "short and sweet" articles about some basic methods we can all use to improve our search engine positioning. Though there are many more complicated methods, these are a great start and can be understood and implemented by anyone.

"How Your Web Site Can Generate Over 25 Times More Buying Customers in Less Than a Year"

by Michael W. Campbell

http://www.1-internet-marketing.com

Get rid of everything on the home page

Put what you now call your home page inside your web site, and use it as a directory to navigate your site. Set up a new home page. Its sole purpose should be to attract a major search engine and funnel the visitors inside, to your site's directory.

> **note** The home page should not contain any frames, tables or scripts of any kind. Use plain simple html consisting of title, headlines, links and body copy, perhaps even a small graphic or two. You don't even need meta tags on the home page.

Use more than one site

Retailers do it in the real world, so why limit yourself to one location in the virtual world? What is hosting going to cost you, $25.00 a month? That's a drip in the ocean compared to the enormous boost in traffic that more sites will bring. Start with six web sites, mirror the content, put slightly different headlines and meta tags on each of the mirrored pages. If your original site consisted of 10 pages, you now have 60 pages working for you in the search engines. Since mirroring is

> **note** Make each site highly targeted to one product line and tie the look and feel of the various sites together by using the same graphic design style and logos.

Chapter 18

being frowned on by some lately, you might want to get around this by making each site into a different product category.

Cross linking

It is very important to make sure each page inside your site (not the home page) links to all your other sites and pages. Each internal page will contain 59 links; the best way to do this is with a 1x1 pixel transparent gif. Doing this will beat the link popularity penalty that's employed by several search engines. It will also create a self-maintaining "stickiness." It doesn't matter if the engine tosses out all your pages except two of them. When it comes to crawl again, the two pages that stuck in the index have links to all your other pages, and the crawler will find them again.

Set up 150 doorway pages (I call them hook pages)

Yes it seems like a lot, but if you have products from 10 manufacturers and they each have 10 different models, that's 100 hook pages per manufacturer or 1000 hook pages in all. Just start with your most popular makes and models, or generic product categories. Make two a week and you'll have over 100 hook pages working for you in the search engines by the end of the year. Will you be accused of

> **note** — Hook pages are my number one source for generating visitors. They work extremely well.

spamming the engine? No. They are not going to penalize you for providing legitimate pages that contain content that people are actually searching for. Do hook pages still work? Yes.

Invert your database

Someone once told you that an online database is a good thing—well, not if you want to be found in the search engines. If your database contains 2000 items, there might be 100 different makes or models and they each have

20 different accessories. Make a static web page for each make or model. That will give you 100 additional highly targeted pages working for you in the search engines. Price changes are easy if your html software is like mine and can make global changes to everything in a folder. Just add an item number or sku number before the price. Then tell your html software to search and replace all instances of that sku number from old to new price.

Submitting an Announcement

Announce only one page per day to each search engine. If you have 60 web pages it will take 60 days. Just be sure to track which pages have been announced to which search engines. If the search engine specifies that only the home page can be submitted, follow the rules—you've been cookied.

Summary

Get more than one site, and mirror the content or put different product categories on each. Just be sure to get domain names with keywords in them. Put up plain home pages—but they'll be search engine beauties—that lead to your "real" home / directory / navigational pages. Cross link everything with invisible pixels. Write two hook pages a week focusing on both generic product categories and specific makes and models. Wait at least 24 hours before submitting another page from the same domain to the search engines.

There, in less than a year, you've gone from one site with 10 pages, to six sites totalling 60 pages, plus 100 hook pages, plus 100 database pages, to a grand total of 260 pages working for you in the search engines. From 10 to 260, that's 26 times more likely to be found, 26 times greater chance of having just the right keyword density to be "flavor of the month." If you follow this simple formula and put in the "sweat equity" required, you'll always have at least 20 top positioned pages in the 8 major search engines at any given moment in time.

Michael W. Campbell is the author of the new Internet marketing book *Nothing But 'Net: How I Generated $750,000 in Internet Revenues in Less Than a Year With Virtually No Advertising Costs.*

Chapter 18

How You Can Nail Top Positioning in All the Search Engines for Simple One- and Two-Word Searches—Even in Ultra Competitive Categories

by Michael Campbell

http://www.1-internet-marketing.com

Here's what I do. I look for bread. Yes, the stuff we eat. To get a top scoring page I look for the simplest of things. I look in a totally non-competitive category like "bread." These pages are not cloaked, switched or stuffed with tricks, they are good basic html pages. They'll tell you exactly what keyword densities are scoring top positions in the search engines right now.

Now, I want to get as much qualified traffic to my home page as possible, so I focus on search phrases consisting of two words. I search for a primary word and a series of secondary words that have real "search potential." These are words that are likely to be used with the primary word in actual searching. This technique allows me to score top position in the search engine for many two word phrases off of a single page.

Here's how it's done. Pick any search engine and search for "bread." The word "bread" becomes the primary word. Then look up "banana bread," "sourdough bread," "corn bread," and so on. Words like "banana, sourdough and corn" become secondary words that will be used along with the primary word in a two word search.

Now examine the html code of the top scoring "bread" pages. You'll discover what keyword and keyword phrase densities are scoring top positioning in that particular search engine right now. For example, you might

259

discover that the primary word needs a density of 5%, or in other words, needs to appear 5% of the time. Examine all the two word searches and you may discover that the secondary words need to appear 2.5% of the time.

Pay careful attention to where the keywords appear in the html code. Notice if they are used in the title, links, headlines and body text. You'll want to create a page with keywords in the same places as the top scoring bread pages. Put the keywords in headlines, body, links and in the title. Also record the total word count on the page and the word count in the page title. Make your web page similar.

Now that you know "the formula" of "real" top scoring html pages, you can apply the same keyword densities, document word count, and document title word count to your competitive category like "cellular phones." Where the word "phones" is the primary word and words like "mobile, digital, pcs, cell and cellular" are the secondary words.

Let's say that we discovered that pages with a word count of around 200 words are working well right now. Using the densities we found earlier means that the word "cellular" must be used exactly 10 times to achieve our 5% density. Each of the other words "mobile, digital, pcs, cell and cellular" must be used exactly 5 times each to achieve our 2.5% density.

Now it becomes a simple matter of writing a very simple web page, with no tricks or expensive gimmicks, no frames, no tables, no JavaScript or bells and whistles of any kind. And it doesn't matter if someone looks for "cellular phones," "digital phones," or "mobile phones" your page will come up in the top ten—the front page of the search engine.

Now if you have more that one web site selling the same thing (which you really should have), you can keep each home page tuned to a different search engine technology. That way, you can have top positioning in all the major search engines for all your top keyword phrases.

Chapter 18

Oh, and if you cross link all your sites with text links or invisible pixels, you'll prevent your pages from getting dropped by some search engines and beat the "link popularity" game that's employed by others.

—Michael Campbell

P.S. I put up an old home page at http://www.phones-cellular.com for you to look at. This exact page was written using the formula above, and in its heyday of Spring '99, was positioned in the top five search results, of the two most popular search engines, for three straight months. This single page was responsible for generating over $35,000.00 in sales.

Michael W. Campbell is the author of the new internet marketing book *Nothing But 'Net: How I Generated $750,000.00 in Internet Revenues in Less Than a Year With Virtually No Advertising Costs*.

Michael's book is just like his articles—full of great information without any "filler" material. If you're serious about playing the search engine game, I highly recommend you get it. (Yes, this is an affiliate link—starting to recognize those now, aren't you!)

http://www.activemarketplace.com/w.cgi?net-1306

As long as I'm plugging Michael's stuff, I may as well tell you about his "Search Engine Commando" software. When you play the search engine positioning game, you have to constantly submit new pages to various search engines. It's time consuming, tedious work.

This software automates the whole process. Point it to your web site pages (on your hard drive) and it compiles a list of web site addresses to submit. You can edit this list if you need to. Once you're happy with the list, turn it loose. It will submit one page to each search engine every 25 hours (this is to prevent the search engine from classifying your submissions as "spam"). Very slick automation.

http://www.activemarketplace.com/w.cgi?sec-1306

One sure thing about search engines is they change. Techniques that yield great positioning in a particular search engine today may not work at all tomorrow—so you'll need to be continually monitoring your positioning.

One of the most popular tools for doing this is "Web Position Gold." Not only does it track your site's position in several search engines, but it helps you build, analyze, and submit search engine friendly pages, plus more. A real "power tool." (Nope, no affiliate link here—I could have, but that many affiliate links in the same section would be stretching my credibility.)

http://webpositiongold.com/

You can get lots of great information about search engine positioning, and just search engines in general at this site:

http://www.SearchEngineWatch.com

For a comparison of various search engines and their rising/falling popularity, check out Michael Campbell's free comparison chart here:

http://www.searchenginepositioning.com

Search engine positioning services

Given the amount of time and effort required to get and maintain good positioning in search engines, it may be to your advantage to pay someone else to do the work. Here are some of the more promising (in my opinion) services:

Bob Massa guarantees top placement in "YAHOO." This is the most coveted prize in all of "searchenginedom." Bob isn't cheap. When I last checked, he charged $2250 + 179/month for his service—but you don't pay if he doesn't produce. Frankly, if you have a site that can convert visitors to customers, this is dirt-cheap.

http://www.magic-city.net

Chapter 18

1st PlaceRanking charges $995 + $99/month and promises to get you at least 10 top 20 placements in the major search engines, within 120 days from the date we begin submitting your pages.

http://1stplaceranking.com

EcomBuffet charges $997 setup + $247/month for 15 top 20 positions in 18 search engines. For 30 top 20 positions it's $1497 + $347/monthly, and for 60 top 20 positions they charge $2497 setup + $447/month. You don't start paying the monthly fee until they get you the agreed upon number of top positions.

http://www.searchenginewebpromotion.com/

Web site design/hosting resources

Web site design/ hosting resources

Though not as "common" as email (yet), web sites are certainly the most *popular* of all Internet-based tools. Have you noticed the proliferation of the prefix "www"? United Parcel Service has www.ups.com on the side of all their delivery trucks. Several magazines have their own web site www address, news stations (television) throw their www address on the screen at the end of news broadcasts—some even take polls via the web.

If people are going to look for you or your product/service on the Internet, they will usually be looking for your web site, not your email address (of course, your email address will be listed on your web site).

> *note* The World Wide Web is growing faster than any other facet of the Internet.

Think of a web site as your own "online" store consisting of one or more web pages. It has its own unique address, and you can use it to showcase your products and/or services in various ways. You can use words, pictures, sound, animation, and video.

Don't use your web site like a billboard—unchanging and boring. Your web site can contain billboards (banners), but they are a lot more than that. Just like a retail storefront, you must make an effort to change things frequently, give it a new look, add products or services, interact with the prospects in some way (drawing, survey, free samples, etcetera). Give people a good reason for coming back to your site, because otherwise it is far too easy for them to leave and never come back.

Your web site may have many functions, including:

- product research
- marketing research
- generating of prospect leads
- customer support and feedback
- online sales (placed directly through your web site)

Let's briefly discuss each one of these:

Product Research: If you are developing a product, you can use your web site to solicit input from your target market. You can get suggestions for new products which are related to the ones you already sell. You can set up a discussion group for buyers of that product, and find out what your customers consider to be its strengths and weaknesses.

Marketing Research: This overlaps product research in some respects. The feedback you receive about your products can help drive new marketing strategies. For instance, if you had previous customers fill out a survey about your product, you might see a pattern in the demographics. You might find that 80% of your customers were middle-income men, age 40-45. You might also find that 60% of your customers enjoyed reading "Mother Earth News."

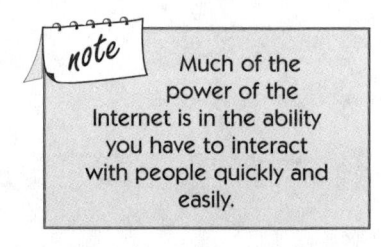

> *note* Much of the power of the Internet is in the ability you have to interact with people quickly and easily.

Chapter 19

This information would be invaluable when planning your next magazine display advertisement campaign. You wouldn't have to use just customers for your marketing research, you could also use any visitors to your site—offer them something free just for filling out a short survey. If they have come to your site and stay for more than 5 seconds, it's because they had at least a passing interest in whatever it is you offer. Find out what kind of people are interested in your site, and find out what other things they have in common!

Another way you can use your site is to test different advertising copy. If you were doing a "direct email" campaign, you could direct half your prospects to one sales message, and direct the other half to a slightly different message—determining which message was better would be a simple exercise of counting orders generated from each one.

Generation of prospect leads: On my first web site, I offered people the opportunity to access over 1300 reports free of charge (most are about making or saving money, but there are some other general interest reports as well). But there was a catch—they had to give me their email address first. Of course you know why—so I could add them to my own "opt-in" email list.

Instead of offering free reports, you might opt to offer a "Tip of the Week" service to anyone that wanted it, via email. Some other people use their web sites to generate phone inquiries, or even to get prospects to come into a showroom and check out the latest model cars—it would only take one car sale to recoup the annual cost of a typical web site.

Customer support and feedback: Besides the feedback mentioned in relation to product/marketing research, you could use your website to disseminate information to your customers upon request 24 hours a day. Several computer and electronics companies have their whole technical support libraries loaded onto a web site at an annual savings of thousands (or millions) of dollars when compared to previous methods.

269

You could set up your own "support" discussion group. You'd find that many of the questions your customers had would be answered by other customers who have had the same problem but found out how to solve it. When this happens, take note, and update your product documentation.

Online Sales: Last but certainly not least, sales are your main goal. Some people use their web site to get online sales exclusively, but I would recommend giving people other options as well. Some people just aren't comfortable entering their personal and credit card information at the computer.

Though people can order "online" through my web site, they are also given the options of ordering by mail, fax, or phone (voice)—and all of these methods have been chosen by my customers. Who knows how many sales I would have missed without offering a variety of ordering options.

The resources listed in this section cover virtually every aspect and consideration of your web site. I've tried to arrange them in a logical order (for instance, discussing domain names before web site design, since you generally want to secure your domain name first thing).

Domain names

For those of you not familiar with this term, a domain name is the root part of your web site address. Another way of looking at it is to think of it as the smallest part of your web address which still differentiates it from any other. For instance, my web site address is "http://www.businesstoolchest.com," and the domain name is "business toolchest.com."

Domain name selection

The bad (or good, depending on how you look at it) thing about domain names is that there's only one of each name. So if you own a donut shop and would like to get a domain name of "donutshop.com," you're out of luck—

someone else already has it. Sometimes you have to be a bit creative. Here are some tools to help you choose one:

At Nameboy, you enter keywords related to your web site, and you're given a list of possible domain names to use. They also tell you if the names are available for registration.

> http://wvww.NameBoy.com

Similar to Nameboy, "Yodon" generates up to 99 possible domain names containing the words you specify. You can also check domain names for availability.

> http://wvww.domain-name-tool.com

AnalogX has a great little software utility (free) you install on your computer. It generates lists of possible domain names to use, and will also check domain names for availability.

> http://www.analogx.com/contents/download/network/whois.htm

HomePageNames has an "advanced" domain name creator.

> http://creator.homepagenames.com/

Unclaimed Domains gives you a frequently updated (I believe daily) list of domain names with expired registrations. Some real gems here.

> http://www.unclaimeddomains.com

At Whois.net you enter keywords and it gives you a list of domain names containing those keywords which have become available for registration

> http://www.whois.net (click on "deleted domain search")

Domain name registration services

There's been a lot of competition to get your domain name registration business, and some companies are really overcharging. Here are three companies I've either used or have had recommended to me by people whose opinions I trust. They're reasonably priced, reputable, and very easy to use.

http://www.kudosnet.com

http://www.joker.com

http://www.000Domains.com

Web hosting

I've had web sites hosted on reliable web host companies as well as unreliable web host companies, so trust me on this: reliable is way better. Sure, you won't get as much practice on your people-skills, but it's worth it. You do not want to be shuffling your web site and domain name from one host company to another.

note — To be successful online, you must use a reliable and scalable web hosting company with excellent customer support. This is critical.

Some of the below recommendations are companies I've used and have been happy with, and some of them are companies who have been recommended to me by people who know what they're talking about, and whom I trust:

http://www.site-works.com

http://www.swdomains.com

http://www.allwebco.com

Chapter 19

http://www.pair.com

http://www.vservers.com

http://www.virtualis.com

http://www.verio.com

http://www.webwizards2000.com

http://www.lazylizard.net

If you want to do some of your own research, here are a couple of good web hosting directories to start with:

http://www.hostindex.com

http://hostsearch.com

By the way, here's a quick tip about choosing from the above selections: decide what software you want to use first. Most people do it backwards—they get an account with a web hosting company, then they start looking around for software that does what they want. Sometimes they find the "perfect" software for their needs only to discover it's not compatible with their web hosting account.

So make sure you know what shopping cart (if any) you want to use, which "scripts" you want to use (more on this later), which affiliate program software you are going to use (if you're going to have an affiliate program), etc. Once you choose your software, you'll know what features your web account must have.

E-Commerce turnkey solutions

Several companies today are touting "one stop shopping" for your e-commerce needs. Their plans include a web site (with varying features), and some offer a merchant account with real-time credit card processing.

273

It's really amazing what these companies will set you up with at such low cost, but always keep in mind the principle of TANSTAAFL. It's something my college professor taught me: *"there ain't no such thing as a free lunch."* Granted, he was talking about feedback and electronic control systems, but it's true here too. You don't get anything without giving up a little of something else. There's always a tradeoff.

Specifically, these setups often limit your flexibility with real-time credit card processing, choice of cart, the use of customized site scripts, etc. To some people that doesn't matter. Make sure you know what you want before you invest too much time in a "simple" solution only to find out it doesn't meet your needs.

http://ncardsystems.com

http://www.go-emerchant.com

http://store.yahoo.com
(includes "SoftGoods" feature (downloadable products))

http://www.bigstep.com

http://www.freemerchant.com

http://www.justwebit.com

http://www.automateyourwebsite.com

Web site design

Should you design your own web pages or let someone else do it? What are the most critical elements of a good design? What makes a web page effective?

Chapter 19

To take a line from *Joe vs. the Volcano*, "Damned if I know, Kimosabe. All I know is when you're making those kind of calls, you're up in the high country." I am not a web designer—I'm a programmer. I don't do graphics. Period. Lucky for me, there are plenty of right-brained people on the internet who do.

One such person is Linda Caroll, and she has graciously agreed to write an article to answer all those questions and more. She even has an illustration.

Designing for success

By Linda Caroll

First impressions

Have you ever watched Alice in Wonderland? Remember the signs? Go here. Go there. This way. That way. Up there. Down here. The sanest thing in that scene was the Hookah-smoking caterpillar. Surrounded by a haze of smoke, he asks, "Whooooo are YOU?" Good question, caterpillar, especially on the Internet. After all, on the Internet, no one knows if you're a dog. Nor does anyone know your age, gender, or your business ethics, for that matter.

The Internet has been dubbed "The Great Equalizer." It's true. With an effective website, it is virtually impossible to differentiate between a large corporation and a small home-based business. The operative word, of course, being "effective." If your website fails to please your visitors, odds are, they'll leave—and they aren't coming back.

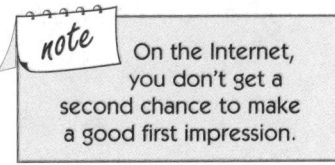

> *note* — On the Internet, you don't get a second chance to make a good first impression.

275

"Buy, buy" versus "Bye-Bye"

What makes a website effective? In a nutshell, a successful website is designed for the customer, with the customer's needs in mind. The majority of websites on the Internet suffer from "Queen of Hearts" syndrome. Remember the Queen of Hearts hollering at Alice? "My way," she bellowed at the top of her lungs. How many times have you seen a website that boldly claimed "best viewed in Internet Explorer," "best viewed in Netscape Navigator," or "best viewed at 800x600"? The viewer is not likely to change their browser or resolution choices to view any one website—nor should they be expected to. It's much easier to move along to the next site.

The sheer volume of websites that don't load properly in all browsers, don't load properly in all screen resolutions, and don't provide an enjoyable experience for the visitor are indications that far too many sites are not really written with the customer in mind. They are written based on the preferences and knowledge of the developer. To make matters worse, there are many website owners who are completely unaware of the fact that their website even has problems loading in other browsers, platforms or screen sizes.

> **note** If the website does not please the visitor, the reaction you are more likely to get is "Bye-Bye"—instead of "Buy, Buy."

The 500 hats of Bartholomew Cubbins?

Should you design your website yourself, or should you hire a developer? The answer lies in your knowledge, and how willing you are to learn new skills.

Have you ever read the Dr. Seuss classic, "The 500 Hats of Bartholomew Cubbins?" Poor Bartholomew has been ordered to take off his hat before the king, but every time he removes a hat, there is another hat still sitting on his head. He removes hat after hat until, finally, Bartholomew reaches the hat to end all hats. A magnificent splendor of a hat. A hat so truly decadent that it

Chapter 19

leaves even the king in awe. So magnificent that it puts the king's crown to shame. Bowing before the king, Bartholomew places the hat on the king's head.

A successful website developer must be a little like Bartholomew Cubbins. That developer must be able to wear the artist's hat in order to develop an eye-catching layout and visual appearance for the website. The developer must then also add the programmer's hat to be able to construct the code for the website so that it loads quickly and consistently across all browsers, platforms and screen resolutions. The developer must also be able to wear the marketer's hat to know what will sell. Add the copywriter's hat, with the ability to write effective copy, and the publicist's hat for knowledge of how to publicize the website, and the promoter's hat in order to be able to promote the site. Under all of those hats, is the one magnificent hat to end all hats—the customer's hat. The customer's hat is the most magnificent of them all because the customer truly is "king."

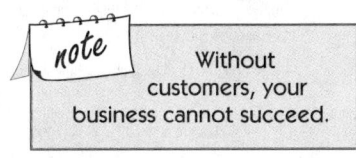

> **note**
> Without customers, your business cannot succeed.

If you are willing to learn to wear all the hats, then by all means—develop your own website. If, however, you do not have the time or the interest, then you need assistance. Whether you learn the skills, pay for those services or barter for them—know that you need all of them in order to succeed. Creating your own site to save the cost of development is not much of a savings, if your site does not bring in customers and generate sales.

Your website is your online substitute for a brick and mortar store. Your potential customers will judge you by your website. They will decide whether or not to buy from you based on your website. They will decide whether or not to even bother contacting you—based on your web site.

Brain pong and spidergrams—planning to succeed

The most important element of design takes place long before the first html tag is typed. Planning. We would all be mortified if a house builder started to build a house without a blueprint. The same rule of thumb should apply to constructing an online business, yet online businesses are constructed without a plan every day. Effective and thorough planning is essential to the success of a website.

Once upon a time, everyone knew that the earth was flat. As time went by, electricity and space travel became the pipe dreams of crazy people. Everyone knew that. Fortunately for us all, there were innovative thinkers. People that were able to "think out of the box." People that shunned conventional thinking and made the impossible—possible.

note — "Thinking out of the box" is an expression that describes nonconformist, creative thinking.

To develop an effective website, you need to be able to determine what the customer wants and needs before the customer asks for it. Before the customer even exists, for that matter. To do that, you need to employ some pretty creative thinking. Successful businesses, and websites, erupt from the minds of people that are able to think out of the box. Like a dormant volcano, the creativity is there, you just need to know how to unleash it.

It's important to know that the human brain does not think "in order." Your mind bounces thoughts and ideas off other thoughts and ideas like a pinball machine, or a game of Pong. A technique frequently used by innovative thinkers is "mind-mapping." Mind-mapping allows you to capture the ideas bouncing around in your head without trying to force them into an ordered list. Making a list constricts innovative thinking and is not nearly as effective or creative.

Chapter 19

Let's say you want to plan a website as a resource center for writers. Draw a circle in the middle of a piece of paper. In the middle of the circle, write "writer's resources." This is the theme of your website.

Next, think of categories, like the departments in a department store. Commercial copywriting, perhaps? Non-fiction? Fiction? Ghostwriting services? Write those down, and link them to the "theme," as illustrated below.

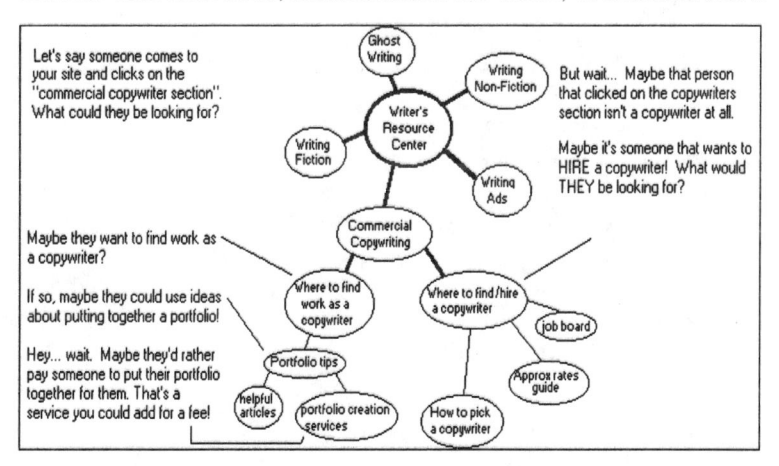

As you look at the spidergram emerging, your mind will bounce. You will find yourself thinking of ideas that spin off the existing ideas. Add them in the appropriate spots. Your mind map might look something like the above illustration.

As you develop your mind map, you will find yourself developing areas of your website. You will also be developing a navigation system that follows each train of thought and corresponds with sections of your website. A smaller website will have a smaller spidergram,

> **note** From the perspective of the future website visitor, there is nothing quite so satisfying as finding a website that has provided exactly what the customer was looking for. You want that to be your site, not your competition's website.

279

or blueprint. For a large website, the spidergram will grow accordingly but will really help you plan ahead for the needs of your potential customers

Testing with figments of your imagination

Many website owners make one very big and costly mistake. They wait until their website is live on the Internet to start the testing process. Don't make that mistake. You can test your blueprint before you construct your website by simply using your imagination.

The human imagination is phenomenal. As children, imaginary friends can be almost as real as a live friend. As an adult, it's in your best interest to recapture the ability to imagine. Actors and actresses do it every day as they mentally get into the role of the character they are playing.

Create an imaginary customer. Give him or her a name and personality. Describe his or her situation. Let's create customers for the writer's resource center that we constructed in our spidergram.

Susan:

Susan is 30 years old and has just had a baby. She has 8 years experience as a corporate copywriter but would like to stay at home to raise her child. She is looking for assistance in finding work in her field that she can do from home. Having been employed in the corporate world, she could probably use some help organizing a portfolio, too.

Bill:

Bill is 54. He owns a small retail store, but also loves to surf the Internet. His copywriter just quit and he needs to find a new copywriter—fast. He's not really sure how to pick a copywriter, because his last copywriter was hired by the previous manager of his store. Bill is open to the idea of hiring someone to work freelance because then he saves paying the employee benefits that he had to pay his last copywriter.

Chapter 19

Create three or four customer profiles. Then, take off the developer's hat and put on the magnificent customer's hat. Pretend. Become your first character and travel through your blueprint assuming the role of the character. Do this with each of the fictional "customers."

Does your website blueprint provide everything that Susan needs? Will she bookmark the site because it is just what she was looking for? What about Bill? Will he find enough information to help him hire a new copywriter? You may discover a few areas that you missed in your first spidergram. These "missed" areas would have been areas in which you dropped the ball in the eyes of your future visitor.

Branding is hot

> **note** While branding is a whole issue unto itself, you do need to consider future branding before you develop and design your website.

Once you have your spidergram in place, it's time to think about branding. Think about some of the biggest companies that you can think of. Would you recognize their logo, or perhaps their slogan? Of course you would. There are very few people in the business world that would not recognize the Windows logo, the AOL logo, and the Visa symbol. The same goes for the Pepsi logo, the Coke logo, and the poppin' fresh Pillsbury Doughboy.

Did you know that people remember 70% of the visual images that they see, and only 30% of the text that they read? So, while excellent copywriting will help you "sell" your image, visual images will also help you make that ever-important first impression.

If you need assistance creating a logo and visual look for your business, you may obtain the services of a graphic designer to help you create your look and logo.

Creating your web site

Armed with your spidergram or blueprint and your new logo, you are ready to start constructing your website. Whether you choose to develop your site yourself, or whether you have your site developed by a developer, there are elements of design that you need to be aware of.

1) Browser Compatibility: Not all code is compatible with all browsers. You will want your website to load in Netscape Navigator, Internet Explorer, WebTv and the current AOL browser. The surest way to verify this is to maintain multiple browsers on your computer, or to use a browser testing service to verify the results. Do not use html testing tools to verify your website's appearance. I have seen testing programs state that a website is compatible with multiple browsers, when in fact the website in question loaded a blank white page in Netscape. Testing software does not have eyes. It cannot "see" what your potential customers will see.

2) Platform Compatibility: Make sure your website loads properly on both Mac and PC platforms. While "html is html" applies to a degree, there are still factors that affect how your website displays on different platforms.

> **note:** Be sure that your website uses a browser safe color palette, not a Windows safe palette.

If you use a Windows-safe palette, many of the colors may not display properly on a Mac because it does not run on Windows. In addition, the font output on a Mac is almost 40% smaller. That means that a size two font, on a Mac, will look 40% smaller than that same size two font on a PC. Not all of your visitors will know how to change the font sizes in their browser. By the same token, if you are designing on a Mac, don't make your fonts too large or they will end up looking even larger, and amateurish, on a PC.

Chapter 19

3) Screen Resolution: With the variety of monitor sizes that are available on the market, you want to ensure that your website displays properly across any screen resolution. There is nothing quite so unprofessional as a website with a tiled background paired with text that is not tabled to fit in the background. Text can become unreadable when it scrolls across a tiled left border. Setting your website in a table can prevent this problem quite easily. You can check your website by changing the resolution of your monitor, or by obtaining software that shows you what your website looks like in various screen resolutions. Be aware, though, that if you have a 19 inch or 21 inch monitor and you set it to a low size like 640x480, your website will look "blown up" and somewhat fuzzy. This is because you are stretching the content to fill a large monitor. People surfing the net with a 14 inch or 15 inch monitor will see the content much more crisp and clear due to their smaller monitor size. The idea is to check layout, not image quality.

4) Fonts: When developing your website, remember that not all people will have the same fonts installed on their computer as you do. If you specify a font style that the viewer does not have installed on their system, the viewer will see a "default" font that looks much like a typewriter font.

As an alternative, specify the font you want, followed by a standard font type. Otherwise, that beautiful flowing Shelley Allegro script will look like something Grandmother pounded out on the typewriter 25 years ago.

> *note* — If you want to ensure that all viewers will see the same fonts that you do, stick to fonts that are default fonts available on most new computers.

5) Colors: According to statistics, most people browse the web with their color settings set to 16 bit color. When developing your website, be sure to use background and font colors selected from the browser safe palette. This will ensure that people actually see the chocolate brown text on a cream background that you intended them to see instead of orange text on a dull green background.

283

In addition, statistics indicate that colors that cause retina strain tend to cause people to leave a website faster. It is not a wise idea to create a website with a brilliant yellow or orange background because the eyestrain will reduce the amount of time anyone spends at your website. The ideal color combinations are black or dark text on a white or pale background, and white or light text on a black or dark background. Using high contrast between your background and your text will also ensure that color blind people will be able to read your site with less eyestrain regardless of the specifics of their visual color limitations.

6) Navigation: Good navigation is crucial. Your navigation system should not change from page to page. After all, when you walk into a store, you want to know that they aren't going to move the exit door on you, don't you? If your potential customers get confused trying to navigate your site, they will usually solve the problem by leaving. In addition to your top of the page navigation, always include a text footer. This has become a standard on the web, and one that people instinctively look for. The text footer becomes doubly important if your upper page navigation uses javascript and the visitor has javascript disabled on their computer system.

> **note:** If your website is extremely large, also include a site map for your viewer's convenience.

7) Images: Many people mistakenly believe that images are the sole reason for slow loading pages. Not true. There are many html creation programs that add so much superfluous code that they create more page bloat than a well-compressed image would cause. However, images should be compressed or diced for quick loading. Ideally, all images on your website should be 10K or smaller. A good image optimization program can reduce the size of most images to acceptable size. Extremely large images can be diced.

Chapter 19

Dicing is simply cutting the image into smaller pieces and re-assembling it in a table. Specify height and width attributes in your image tag, too. The height and width attributes will allow your images to load much more quickly and efficiently because they "tell" the browser how much space to leave for the image. Have you ever seen a website where the text jumps around until the page has fully loaded? In most cases, that happens because the browser does not "know" how much room to leave for the image until the image has finished loading.

In addition, remember to specify a name for the image in the "alt" tag. This provides a description for the occasional surfer who may have their images turned off. In addition, if you choose your image names carefully, they will be helpful to you when the search engines index your website.

Summary: Web site do's and don'ts

1) Winning Elements: The number one element of a winning site is visitor value. Several issues go hand in hand with visitor value. Does the site load quickly? Is it browser, resolution and platform compatible? Is it easy to navigate? Does it make an impression?

- All pages should load in 25 seconds or less.

- All pages will be compatible with Netscape versions 4 and 6, IE4, IE5, as well as the current AOL browser and WebTv.

- All pages should be compatible with all screen resolutions.

- All pages should be compatible with both Mac & PC platforms.

- All pages should be compatible with AOL's image extension.

- All fonts should be compatible with default computer fonts.

- All images should be optimized, compressed and/or diced for super-fast load time.

285

2) **Red Flags:** Avoid these like the plague.

- **Lack of real content:** Too many sites are nothing but glorified sales letters that do not offer any help or information. Businesses that are "helpful" and provide information have a higher success rate than "sales letter" sites or sites that are little more than a collection of banners and buttons.

- **Under construction pages:** As a rule of thumb, if it's not ready, don't put it online. People don't bookmark unfinished pages to come back later. They just get disappointed and move on.

- **Inconsistent layout:** Have you ever clicked a link and wondered if you were still at the same site? Maintain consistency to make your visitors comfortable.

- **Spelling and html mistakes:** If your website does not look professional and contains spelling, grammar or html mistakes, people will make a subconscious parallel assumption about your business, assuming that you are not very professional, either.

- **Frames:** If you're not an html wizard, you run the risk of frames that don't display all the content, or that do not fit the viewer's monitor resolution. Worse yet, search engines can't index frames properly and people may find your interior frames listed in a search engine— without any of the navigational information that is in "another" frame.

- **Long download time:** If you think they will wait—they won't.

- **Dead links, awkward navigation, and complicated ordering instructions:** All drive traffic away from a site.

Chapter 19

The secret to website success

Your website can be your most faithful employee. It can greet your customers, answer their questions and process their orders—24 hours a day, 365 days a year. Despite the popularity of all the "Insider's Secrets" programs out there, I don't believe success is a secret. Success is a gift that people give you in return for what you have given them.

Resource Info:
Linda Caroll is an award winning website developer and columnist. Her clients include well-known Internet marketers, celebrities, large corporations and small home businesses. Publications include: "Html Is Not Rocket Science," " Success. The Road Less Travelled?," "The Shocking Truth About Internet Marketing" and more. You may visit Ms. Caroll's website at http://www.LindaCaroll.com

Recommended web site designers

Here are a few designers I can recommend—all of them listen carefully to their client, then punch out a great looking design based on their input. Besides that, they're just plain nice.

Linda Caroll   http://www.lindacaroll.com

Kristy Tamsevicius   http://www.kcustom.com

Catherine Samir   csamir@cyberclick.com

Peter Grice   http://www.internationalhosting.com/cwd/

By the way, I know it's a bit odd that Catherine doesn't have a web site for showcasing her work, but I'll personally vouch for her experience and the quality of her work. Send her an email and she'll give you the URLs of a few of her recent jobs.

Resources for designing your own web site

If you decide to do your own web design, there are tons of great resources to help you do it right. I have listed quite a few below, but it's still just the tip of the iceberg.

HTML tutorials

Though there's lots of software for making your web site "without knowing HTML," I recommend you learn at least the basics—it will help you tremendously when you find it necessary to "tweak" your web site. Some of the below resources actually talk about a lot more than HTML, so check out the other links on the pages.

http://www.coolnerds.com

http://htmlgoodies.earthweb.com/

http://www.ncsa.uiuc.edu/General/Internet/WWW/HTMLPrimer.html

http://wdvl.internet.com/Authoring/

http://www.mediabuilder.com/webdesigntutor.html

http://home.cnet.com/webbuilding/0-3880.html

HTML validators/checkers

http://www2.imagiware.com/RxHTMLz

http://validator.w3.org

http://www.weblint.org/gateways.html

Chapter 19

Free HTML editors

These aren't as feature-rich as the for-pay software, but they'll get you up and running quickly and with no cost.

>http://www.aolpress.com

>http://www.altheim.com/equinox/htmledit   (for Mac computers)

>http://www.arachnoid.com/arachnophilia

>http://www.cuteftp.com/products/cutehtml

HTML editors

Here are several of the most popular web editors. These have many more features than the free software above, but they cost money and generally require more time to learn.

Web Express:	http://www.mvd.com/webexpress/index.htm
Namo:	http://www.namo.com
NetObjects Fusion:	http://www.netobjects.com
FrontPage:	http://www.microsoft.com/frontpage
DreamWeaver:	http://www.macromedia.com/software/dreamweaver

Website templates

If you have a hard time creating a "look and feel" without some help, these templates will save you lots of time. Some are free, and some cost money.

289

http://www.1001designs.com

http://www.faystudios.com/webplates.html

http://www.freesitetemplates.com

Image / graphics libraries

If you don't have the time or budget to create custom images for your own site, don't despair—the following image libraries contain thousands of images you can use on your site. Be sure to check the use policy before you grab any images—most are free, but that's always subject to change.

http://www.iconbank.com/gx/index.htm

http://www.flamingtext.com

http://www.stars.com/Vlib/Multimedia/Images_and_Icons.html

(Directory to free or almost free image collections)

Online graphic/image generators

There are several sites where you can button / text images right from your web browser. On others you can apply special effects to images you already have on your website.

http://www.buttontool.com

http://www.cooltext.com

http://nbswebfx.com

[Several special effects on images you have online]

This one has lots of tools, including the following: 3D Text Maker, Animated Banner Maker, ButtonMaker and more:

>http://www.mediabuilder.com

Online banner creation tools

>http://www.wealthworld.com/bannertools.htm
>
>http://web-animator.com/
>
>http://www.bannerforge.com/
>
>http://www.webgfx.ch/titlepic.htm
>
>http://www.quickbanner.com
>
>http://www.animation.com
>
>http://www.crecon.com/banners

Online web form creator tools

Not only do these services help you create your own online form (which your visitors use to send you information per your request), but they store the submitted form data in a database which you can access as needed.

>http://www.formsite.com

Web site search utilities

If you have many pages of content on your site, a "site search" utility may be very helpful to your visitors. It will also help you to determine what people are looking for when they come to your site—valuable information. Here are some services you can use to easily implement a search utility on your site:

http://pinpoint.netcreations.com

http://www.atomz.com

http://www.freefind.com

http://www.picosearch.com

Web site content resources

The following sites have tons of articles you can use as "content" on your site. These aren't articles from those old worn-out "Reprint Rights" disks or CD-ROMs. These are high quality articles written by people who know what they're talking about.

Be sure to check the requirements for your use. You usually need to send an email explaining which articles you're using, and where you'll be placing them.

WWIO: http://www.certificate.net/wwio

Dr. Kevin Nunley: http://www.drnunley.com/MARKET.htm

Michel Fortin: http://www.success-doctor.com/archive.htm

Jim Daniels: http://www.bizweb2000.com/articles.htm

Terry Dean: http://www.bizpromo.com/free

Here's another site to check out. Unlike the above sites, however, this site does not give you the rights to reproduce the articles. However, each article contains the author's contact information. My suggestion is that you email the author of any article(s) you wish to use on your web site and see if they will allow it.

MakingProfit.com: http://www.makingprofit.com

Want automatically updating content related to your web site's theme? Here are a couple of places to get it. All you have to do is copy some HTML code (JavaScript, actually) where you want the "content" to show up on your web page. You don't do anything after that—content is updated as often as every 15 minutes.

iSyndicate: http://www.isyndicate.com

ScreamingMedia: http://www.screamingmedia.com

Web site checking

Once it's designed, these tools will analyze your site and report any problems such as HTML errors, slow-loading pages, invalid links, etc.

http://www.netmechanic.com

http://www.websitegarage.com

Tracert.com is a nifty service that tells you how long your site takes to download from different parts of the world:

http://tracert.com

Web site monitoring

You'll want to maintain a constant vigil on your web site—if something stops working, you need to fix it before it costs you too much business. Obviously you can't afford to spend all your time clicking over to your web site just to make sure it's working—and that's where these tools come in. They'll do the monitoring for you, and will alert you if there are any problems.

http://www.globalsitemonitor.com

http://www.netwhistle.com

http://www.webpartner.com

http://www.redalert.com

http://watchdog.mycomputer.com

http://www.netmechanic.com/

SevenTwentyFour is a little different than the above services—it's a link-checking service. Not only does it check the links on your site to make sure the specified URLs are valid, it checks links pointing TO your site too. So if someone has an error in their link to your site, you'll be notified.

http://www.seventwentyfour.com

Web site traffic analysis/statistics

To maximize your profit potential you need frequent, accurate, and detailed statistics about your web site traffic. With the right information, you can tell which of your advertising campaigns are working, and which are not. You'll be able to calculate the value of a visitor, the conversion rate of your various sales pages, and more.

Some web hosting companies have excellent web site traffic analysis included with your account, and some don't. If yours doesn't, or if you want even more details than what your existing traffic analysis package offers, check out the following services:

> **note** — When you observe a change in the traffic to a particular page, you can adjust your online marketing strategy accordingly, and you'll enjoy steadily rising revenues.

Chapter 19

Hitometer:	http://websitegarage.netscape.com/ turbocharge/ hitometerIndex.html
SuperStats:	http://www.superstats.com
HitBox:	http://www.hitbox.com
WebTrendsLive:	http://www.webtrendslive.com/default.htm

(Allows you to monitor right through the ordering process.)

OpenWebScope:	http://www.openwebscope.com
Gumball:	http://www.gumball-tracker.com
SiteGauge:	http://www.sitegauge.com/

Web site advertising tracking

In many cases, one of the above traffic statistics services will be all you need for tracking your advertising. However, there are a few programs designed for this purpose alone, and there may be some advantages in using them:

Roibot:	http://www.roibot.com
ProLinkz:	http://prolinkz.com
ClickIt:	http:// www.1-promote.com/1-promote/ main.html
Ultimate Ad Tracker:	http://ultimateadtracker.com

Adding interactivity to your web site

I'm using the broad sense of the word "interactive" here. I'm talking about anything you add to your web site which requires input from your visitors. Things like polls, discussion boards, "recommend this site to a friend" pages, and more.

These things help your marketing efforts in a number of ways. They increase the "stickiness" of your site (making people want to come back), they increase your word-of-mouth advertising, and they help you build your opt-in list(s).

Website interactivity tool collections

Several companies provide a number of "interactive devices" you can include on your web site. Some services are free (usually the tradeoff is some kind of advertising), and some cost a little money, but not too much.

http://www.mycomputer.com

http://www.bravenet.com

http://liveuniverse.com/world

http://www.sitegadgets.com

http://www.beseen.com

http://www.vantagenet.com

Chapter 19

Discussion board (forum) services and software

There aren't many tools better than the discussion board for bringing people back to your site again and again. Like many other things on the internet, you have two choices: you can install software on your web server, or you can use a service.

Software:

http://awsd.com/scripts/webbbs

http://www.infopop.com/

http://netbula.com/anyboard/

Services:

http://www.bravenet.com

http://www.network54.com

http://www.centerwheel.com/index.html

http://www.smartgroups.com/

http://www.beseen.com/board/itw_beseen.html

Polls/surveys

These services allow you to run your own poll or survey. Here's an idea—run a survey related to your product/service. Once you get 1000 respondents or so, compose and send out a snappy press release.

http://www.pollit.com

297

http://www.insta-poll.com

http://www.mrpoll.com

http://www.surveymonkey.com

http://www.cpulse.com

These last two add a little extra. You can have them conduct the survey even without having your own list of potential respondents. They have a database of people meeting your demographic requirements who will fill out your survey. With Zoomerang, this is an option. With InsightExpress it's a requirement. This extra service costs more, of course.

http://www.zoomerang.com

http://www.insightexpress.com

Recommend-to-a-friend

Word of mouth is still the best advertising—that's why viral marketing works so well. These resources allow you to put a "recommend this site to a friend" link or button on your site. The first is a service, the other two are links to software you install on your server. All are free.

Let-em-Know:	http://www.letemknow.com
BirdCast:	http://bignosebird.com/cgi.shtml
Master Recommend:	http://willmaster.com/master/recommend
Constant Contact:	http://www.constantcontact.com
	(they offer a suite of services)

Chapter 19

Chat rooms

Many web hosting companies include "chat room" services as part of your account. But if not, try these services:

http://www.talkcity.com

http://www.beseen.com

Your own auction

Internet Auctions are very popular. Here are a couple ways to add one to your own site. The first link is to software you install on your own site, the second link is to an "auction content service" which you can integrate with your own site.

http://www.everysoft.com/auction.html

http://ep.com/

Currency conversion utility

If you're going to be selling to people outside your own country, adding this little currency conversion utility will certainly aid your foreign customers.

http://www.xe.com

299

Web site promotion

20

Web site promotion

The resources you'd expect to find in this section have already been included in the "Advertising" and "Search Engine Promotion" sections. However, the subject is so critical to your online success I wanted to include a couple of articles in this section to reemphasize its importance.

Both of these articles are from acknowledged authorities, and I expect anyone could be successful just by applying the information in them. You'll probably notice some of the resources in Allan Gardyne's article are listed earlier in this guide, but many aren't.

Article 1: The Internet Marketer's Mini-Checklist

Michel Fortin

Throughout my online travels, and particularly in my marketing consulting practice, I encounter many a netpreneur who wonder about the reasons why they are not yet successful." Mike, why am I not getting as many hits?" or "as many sales?" they ask.

It's a question I am asked all too often, it seems.

I can appreciate their frustration since I've been there. It took me years to achieve what I'm experiencing today, and a lot of it is the result of pure trial and error. But a lot of it is also based on simple, common sense. The reality, however, is that so many people, enticed by the overblown hype and promises of the web, expect some "get rick quick" solution.

I wish there was one.

So I often reply with a checklist, which I will reprint in this week's editorial. It is far from being a comprehensive list—there are many more tactics, techniques and strategies one can implement beyond what the list suggests. Additionally, for many it might appear as an appropriate roadmap for the newbie webmarketer. Some tend to even scoff at its simplicity.

But surprisingly, its simplicity is the reason why it is also so easily ignored by the more experienced. I ask that you take a good, hard look at it. Answer it truthfully and completely. How many of the tactics suggested did you really implement? How many have you abandoned after only a few attempts? And how many tactics do you put into action on a regular basis?

Think about your answers.

Granted, some of these may not apply to all situations. But generally, I have found that those who complain the most have not implemented a fraction of these, or lack a clear plan of action through which some of the most profitable among these should be repeated on a periodic basis. The latter is crucial.

My colleague Jim Daniels of http://www.bizweb2000.com/ is the master when it comes to developing and maintaining a rigorous marketing plan. (Jim printed his own in a recent issue of his very informative BizWeb Gazette as a template that's worth its weight in gold.) So let me ask you at this point: isn't it time you, too, have one—and consistently stick to it?

So here is the checklist:

✓ Are you subscribed to ezines and websites (like IMC's own at http://www.marketingchallenge.com/) on Internet marketing, and do you read/visit them on a daily basis?

Chapter 20

✓ Have you implemented most if not some of the ideas you've learned in them? What were your results? Good? Bad? Why?

✓ What ideas worked best for you? What ideas worked least? Do you or did you track your results? How? Do you review and analyze them on a daily basis? What are they telling you?

✓ Do you constantly educate yourself on your industry and your specific area of expertise? In fact, do people look upon you as an expert in what you do?

✓ Do you "love" what you do?

✓ Do you follow a daily marketing regimen? Consistently? If so, what did you do this week? And the week before that?

✓ Did you bid on keywords on http://www.Goto.com? Which ones? Did you try other pay-per-rank engines? Did you use their keyword suggestion tools and look at different variations?

✓ Do you have an affiliate program for your products? If not, have you implemented another form of "viral" marketing?

✓ Does your web site have tools to help make it "sticky"? For example, do you maintain a discussion forum? A site-specific search tool? An archive of informative content?

✓ Does your business model strive for quantity or quality? In other words, do you seek bigger profits or market share? Are you achieving it or do you seem to be achieving the other?

✓ What areas of your business need improvement? An even more important question to ask is what do your customers think?

✓ Do you tweak and test your web site copy on a consistent basis?

- ✓ Do you maintain an opt-in list or regularly publish an ezine? Do you remain in constant contact with subscribers?

- ✓ Does your marketing include increasing your subscriber base?

- ✓ Do you continually research your customers, your product category, your industry, and especially your competition?

- ✓ What makes you unique? What's your USP (i.e., your unique selling proposition)? In other words (and think about this), what's your single, most marketable, competitive edge?

- ✓ Do you communicate that edge in all that you do?

- ✓ Did you submit your site to the major search engines and niche-specific engines? Do you monitor your rankings?

- ✓ Have you written articles and submitted them to newsletters read specifically by your target market? Do you periodically write and distribute press releases? How many? To whom?

- ✓ Do you market and advertise offline? If so, where?

- ✓ Do you have a good, compelling email signature file? And do you use it with every piece of correspondence you make?

- ✓ Do you participate in newsgroups? Message boards? Forums? And especially those frequented by your target market?

- ✓ Do you offer one, two or three products? In other words, how focused are you on your niche or on your perfect customer?

- ✓ In fact, who is your perfect customer? Do you know your product's demographics (e.g., age, gender, employment, etc.), geographics (e.g., location, country, city, etc.) and psychographics (e.g., interests, culture, lifestyle, etc.)?

Chapter 20

✓ And do you have any back-end products or services with which you can upsell your customer base? If not, do you (or could you) offer products from non-competing strategic alliances?

✓ Is your ecommerce system a well-oiled machine? Do you accept credit cards on your site? What other payment options do you provide? Do you have a customer support number or email?

✓ Do you package or bundle your products in order to increase their perceived value? Do you offer alternative packages (maybe with different price points or additional services)?

✓ Do you have a top level domain name (yourname.com)? Does it invoke the core benefit or if not at least the nature of your site? Is it easy to pronounce? Spell? Remember?

✓ Do you have any strategic marketing alliances in place?

✓ In fact, how many alliances do you have in place? Do you keep in constant contact with them? What about joint ventures? Cross promotions? Referrals networks?

✓ Is your site easy to navigate? Read? Download? Do you provide your visitors with good, fresh, updated content?

✓ Most of all, do you give visitors a reason to come back?

✓ Have you implemented an automated referral system on your site (like IMC's http://www.letemknow.com/) that visitors can use to easily refer your site to others?

✓ Do you have testimonials on your site? A strong guarantee? A bonus offer? A privacy and security policy? An FAQ page?

✓ Do you sell advertising on your site? In your ezine? If so, did you develop a media kit for potential advertisers?

✓ Have you advertised online? In which ezines? On which sites? Do you constantly tweak your ad copy and track your results?

✓ Have you participated on online talk shows? Chat specials?

✓ Have you expanded your mind in terms of looking at different places, as many places as possible, in which you can market your site and where your target market likely congregates?

✓ In fact, do you try to keep your site, its address, or its offers in front of your target market's eyeballs? How often?

✓ Does your site copy invite people to surf deeper into it? Or is it laced with external links that drive people out?

✓ Do you conduct contests? Draws? Surveys? Does your site capture, with permission, the email addresses of your visitors, especially on the first page, "above the fold?"

✓ Do you swap ezine ads with other publishers? Or in the very least, do you have a reciprocal linking strategy in place?

As you can see, this list can go on. But in my experience, just the above could open some eyes. For example, with my own copywriting service (see http://SuccessDoctor.com/copy.htm), my clients must fill out a similar (but more extensive) list of questions before any work commences. As I found, simply answering it has been quite insightful for many.

Ultimately, you would be surprised to find out how much it pays to go back to the basics. Regularly. Consistently.

Michel Fortin is a speaker, author, web copywriter, college professor and ebusiness consultant. He is also the editor of the Internet Marketing Chronicles, delivered weekly to over 100,000 subscribers. FREE business articles, an ebook and a newsletter subscription at http://SuccessDoctor.com/

Chapter 20

Article 2: 65 Ways to Boost Your Web Traffic

Allan Gardyne

An obvious newcomer to the Net asked me recently whether he ought to buy Corey Rudl's marketing course. "After all," he said, "there are only a few ways to promote your site."

As experienced e-marketers know, there are hundreds of ways to promote your site.

Jody McPhee of http://www.TrekPlanet.com got me started on this project when she published a checklist of marketing ideas. I've expanded Jody's list and added good URLs I've found for advice and resources.

How many of these 65 traffic-boosting techniques do you use?

Search engines:

Danny Sullivan's Search Engine Report

   http://searchenginewatch.com/about/subscribe.html

One click submits your site to the 8 top search engines

   http://www.all4one.com/all4submit/

(I tried All4one.com and it worked well—it verifies that the submission was made successfully.)

   http://www.mmgco.com/wsrev195.html

   http://www.searchengine-news.com/

   http://www.virtualfreesites.com/search.html

   http://www.searchenginewatch.com/

http://www.jimtools.com

http://www.virtualpromote.com/promoteb.html

http://www.realnames.com/

Pay-per-click search engines:

http://www.PayPerClickSearchEngines.com

Directories:

http://search.yahoo.com/bin/search?p=directories

Reciprocal Links:

http://www.sev.com.au/webzone/announce/networking.htm

http://www.igoldrush.com/missing/

http://iwr.com/free/reciprocal.htm

http://www.reciprocallink.com/

http://www.fraternet.com/zel/

Web Rings:

http://1x.com/advisor/maher19.htm - advice

http://www.webring.org/

http://www.ringsurf.com/

Message boards—Join in Discussions:

http://www.forumone.com

Chapter 20

http://webwizards.net/AssociatePrograms/discus/

http://bizweb2000.com/wwwboard/

http://www.virtualpromote.com/

http://homebasedbusiness.com/cgibin/index.cgi

http://www.talkbiz.com

http://www.ablake.net/forum/

http://www.profitlines.com/ipub

http://www.free-publicity.com/cgi-bin/talk.cgi

Message boards—setting up your own:

http://www.cgi-resources.com

Discus—the one used by AssociatePrograms.com

http://www.chem.hope.edu/discus

Guest Books:

http://www.freecenter.com/guestbook.html

Awards:

Earning awards for your web site

http://www.focusa.com/articles/earn_awards1.htm

311

Press releases:

How to Get the Press on Your Side by Shel Horowitz

http://www.frugalfun.com/press.html

http://www.automatedpr.com

http://www.promotionworld.com/directory/press.shtml

http://www.prnewswire.com/

http://www.gebbieinc.com/

http://www.mrsmithmedia.com

Banners:

http://www.markwelch.com/web_ads.htm

http://www.BannerTips.com

http://www.smartage.com/promote/smartclicks/index2.html

http://www.BannerWorkz.com

Banner exchanges:

http://www.freecenter.com/bannerx.html

http://www.promotionworld.com/be/worth.shtml

http://www.adbility.com

E-zine advertising (huge list of places which list newsletters):

http://www.satcom.net.au/success/newsletter.html

Chapter 20

http://www.directmarketing-online.com/features/
archives/articles/10211998.htm

http://www.lifestylespub.com

Get listed on "What's Hot" and "What's Cool" Sites:

http://www.sev.com.au

http://www.stpt.com/

http://www.emazing.com/

"What's New" sites:

http://www.sev.com.au/webzone/announce/whatsnew.htm

http://www.webmagnet.com/htdi.html#whatsnew

URL Plates:

http://www.iditplates.net

Word of mouth:

Business cards—15 ways to use your business cards as a marketing tool

http://www.smartbiz.com/sbs/arts/sbs4.htm

E-mail (E-mail help for the newcomer):

http://everythingemail.net/email_help_tips.html

Chat rooms:

http://sbinformation.miningco.com/mpchat.htm

313

Chat Directory:

http://www.topica.com

ICQ: The ICQ E-mail Directory:

http://www.icq.com/search/email.html

Newspaper articles:

Read this article by Gary Lockwood

http://www.bizsuccess.com/articles/

Write killer news releases

http://www.netrageousresults.com/PR/pressrelease.html

Magazine articles (thousands of magazines, hundreds of newspapers):

http://www.mrsmithmedia.com

Online articles (provide articles for webmasters and ezine publishers):

http://bizweb2000.com/articles.htm

Email help for the newcomer:

http://everythingemail.net/emailtips.html

Ezine Articles:

http://www.meer.net/~johnl/e-zine-list/keywords/

http://www.ezine-universe.com/

Chapter 20

Newspaper adverts:

http://www.bonafideclassifieds.com/

TV adverts, Radio adverts, Radio talkshows:

http://www.radiospace.com/programs.htm#Contents

Magazine adverts, E-mail signatures:

http://www.bizweb2000.com/sigfile.htm

How to design a .sig file:

http://www.webbers.com/emark/sigfiles-nick-nichols.html

Free classified ads:

http://classifieds.yahoo.com/

Your own classified ad page:

http://ep.com/

Ezine ad swaps:

http://www.list-city.com/

Publish your own newsletter and promote it:

http://www.wilsonweb.com/articles/majordomo.htm

http://www.advertgising.com/newsletter

http://communitybuilding.com/

http://www.satcom.net.au/success/newsletter.html

315

Pay for newsletter subscribers:

http://www.signupsales.com/

Opt-in e-mail announcements:

http://www.postmasterdirect.com

http://www.BulletMail.com

http://www.wilsonweb.com/webmarket/lists.htm

Give away products at other sites:

http://www.uniques.com/

Start your own revenue sharing program:

http://www.AssociatePrograms.com/search/howto.shtml

Run a seminar:

http://www.gapent.com/seminars/

Send postcards:

http://www.Netcards.com

http://www.wbcards.com

Distribute car stickers, magnets, etc.:

http://www.websticker.com/

Newsgroups:

http://www.dejanews.com

Chapter 20

The best ones for free ads:

   http://www.drnunley.com/

Marketing on newsgroups:

   http://www.bizweb2000.com/newsgrou.htm

Join a mall:

   http://AShoppingGuide.com

The truth about Internet malls:

   http://www.netrageousresults.com/reports/thetruth.html

Offer digital postcards:

   http://www.all-yours.net/postcard/

Recommend-it:

   http://www.recommend-it.com/

Jim Rhodes' free referral script:

   http://deadlock.com/promote/

Capitalize on news events:

   http://www.promotionworld.com/ideas/hits.shtml

Help visitors return:

   http://www.netmind.com/html/users.html

   http://www.micromat.com/

317

Create a community:

http://communitybuilding.com/

Work with charities:

http://www.drnunley.com/

Join discussion lists:

http://www.listtool.com

http://www.paml.net

http://www.lsoft.com/lists/listref.html

http://wwwtopica.com/

Networking (tips from the queen of networking):

http://www.profnet.org

Give a speech:

Make a speech and live to tell about it

http://www.bizsuccess.com/august97.htm

Bumper sticker on your car, jewelry with your web site logo on it, cap or t-shirt with your web site on it:

http://www.Hatsurf.com

Public relations (tips for press release writing and effective media relations):

http://www.newsbureau.com/tips/

Chapter 20

Learn from the experts:

http://www.netrageousresults.com/PR/index.html

Public relations online resources and organizations:

http://www.webcom.com/impulse/resource.html

Run sweepstakes:

http://www.onlinesweeps.com/articles/promo.html

http://www.arentfox.com/features/sweepstakes/

http://www.webcontests.com/bestsweeps.html

Hold contests:

http://contests.about.com

http://www.sev.com.au/

Create a media kit and post it here:

http://www.searchz.com/mediakits

Add interactivity to encourage repeat visitors, add chat, message boards, surveys, guest books, games, postcards, search engines, auctions, etc.:

http://www.cgi-resources.com

Make friends—and they will publicize your site (good news spreads like wildfire):

http://www.AssociatePrograms.com/search/newsletter047.shtml

Joint ventures:

The most powerful marketing concept on earth

http://www.jvmarketer.com/jvcenter.html

Powwow—brainstorm, mind map, think up brilliant new ideas

Here are some offbeat offline ones.

http://www.inc.com/

Because so many new people are coming on the Internet all the time and being seduced by get-rich-quick advertising, there's a place for a marketing advice section on just about any site.

Feel free to post this list on your website or use it in your newsletter. You could add your own favorite links to it, and also add full descriptions of each site to make it more useful for your visitors.

You could also offer it free via an autoresponder, including a link to your site or newsletter, of course.

Allan Gardyne owns AssociatePrograms.com, a comprehensive directory of affiliate programs. His free Associate Programs Newsletter has been named top marketing newsletter on the Internet by BestEzines.com. To subscribe, just send a blank e-mail to: *associateprog@add.postmastergeneral.com*

Web site software resources

21

Web site software resources

Just about every section of this guide has links to software resources related to the topic discussed therein. In this section I have included links to software resources of a more general nature (but still related to your web site).

CGI Scripts

CGI is short for "Common Gateway Interface," and "scripts" is just another word for "programs." CGI scripts are programs that run on your web server. For instance, when you submit an order form on a web site, that data is sent to a CGI script/program. The program logs your order information to a file, sends out a receipt email, and anything else it was designed to do, then sends a "thank you" page to your browser.

Most (if not all) of the software packages in the "interactivity" subsection of the "Web Site Design" section are CGI programs. There are thousands of free CGI programs, and thousands more "for pay" programs. Sometimes the free ones are as good or better than the programs that cost you money, but you generally get better customer support with the programs you pay for.

Here are several places to find these programs—the first two resources may be all you ever need if you're just looking for free programs, but the others resources have some great software, too!

323

http://scriptsearch.internet.com

http://cgi-resources.com

http://www.freecode.com

http://www.cgitoolbox.com

http://www.willmaster.com

http://www.webmaster-base.com

http://newmillennium.net

http://solutionscripts.com

http://www.freewareweb.com

http://www.lakeweb.com/scripts/begin.html

http://www.webthing.com/tutorials/cgifaq.html

http://www.boutell.com/faq/cgiprob.htm

http://www.extropia.com

http://www.speakeasy.org/~cgires/cgi-tips.html

http://www.worldwidemart.com/scripts

http://www.superscripts.com

Custom software

Sometimes there's no existing application that will meet your specific needs. In such cases, a custom solution is required. Custom software can be surprisingly affordable. The below resources will help to match your custom programming need to a programmer.

I've used eLance.com a number of times myself, and have always been very pleased with the caliber of the software and service I received.

Elance: http://www.elance.com

Guru.com: http://www.guru.com/

CGI-Resource: http://cgi.resourceindex.com/Programmers/

Index

A-Con♦♦♦♦

Ad strategies 38
Advertising promotion 26
Affiliate program banners 40
Affiliate program services 76
Affiliate program software 77
Anti-cracking software 101
Anti-virus software 100
Article submission/distribution .. 62
Autoresponders 130
Background checks 190
Banner advertising 44
Banners 38
Barter 191
Branding 29, 281
Browser compatibility 282
Bulletin boards 107
Business intelligence 244
Business web sites 198
CGI scripts 323
Chat rooms 299
Children's Online Privacy
  Protection Act (COPPA) 173, 185
Clickthroughs 71
Colors 283
Competitive intelligence 244
Competitor intelligence 244
Content conversion 191

Cop-Ex♦♦♦♦

Copywriters 192
Co-Ventures 154
Cross linking 257
CPC (cost per click) 30
CPM (cost per thousand) 29
CPS (cost per sale) 31
Credit card fraud protection ... 212
Currency conversion 299
Custom software 324
Customer support and
  feedback 269
Customer support tools 87
Discussion board 297
Discussion groups 107
Discussion lists 232
Disk failure 102
Domain name selection 270
Domain names 270
Doorway pages 257
Download sites 194
Ebooks (electronic books) 113
Electronic checks 212
Electronic newsletters 233
Email merging 129
Email robot 130
Expert sites 239

327

Ez-O♦♦♦♦

Ezines	135
Ezine advertising	57
Fax broadcasting	85
Fax-on-demand	83
Fonts	283
Forums	107
Free Internet access	189
Hits	71
Hook pages	257
ICQ	198
Images	284
Instant message	87
Interactivity	296
Internet marketing	148
Internet phone	86
Joint ventures	154
Link exchange banners	39
List servers	128
Magazines	238
Marketing research	268
Mass appeal test	183
Merchant account	204
Navigation	284
Newsfeeds	236
Online printing/duplication services	195
Online sales	270
Opt-in email advertising	58
Order fulfillment	145

P-Ta♦♦♦♦

Paid advertising banners	41
Payment processing service	206
Pay-per-action advertising	56
Pay-per-click search engines	47
PDF files	113
Platform compatibility	282
Polls/surveys	297
Post card marketing	196
Press releases	60
Privacy	196
Private information	178
Product research	268
Productivity tools	121
Prospect leads	269
Qualifiers	31
Real-time services	206
Registration services	272
Screen resolution	283
Search engines	230
Search engines/directories	242
Search engine positioning	259
Sequential email services	131
Sequential email software	131
Snail mail	90
Spam	58
Strategic intelligence	244
Surge suppressors	96
Sweepstakes/contests	64
TANSTAAFL	274
Targeted response bots	235
Targeting	28

TE-W♦♦♦♦

Text editors 193
Traffic analysis/statistics 294
UCE (unsolicited commercial
    email) 58
UL (Underwriters Laboratories)..97
UPS (uninterruptible power
    supply) 99
USPS mail online 91
Unique visits 71
Viral marketing 197
Virtual assistants 189
VoiceMail and FAX services 81
Web hosting 272
Web sites
    checking 293
    content resources 292
    design 274
    design/hosting 267
    monitoring 293
    search utilities 291
    ranked 199
Workshops/Seminars/
    Trade shows 239